Coastal
Beauty

Wildflowers and Flowering Shrubs of
Coastal British Columbia and Vancouver Island

Neil L. Jennings

Rocky
Mountain Books

VANCOUVER • VICTORIA • CALGARY

Rocky Mountain Books
#108 – 17665 66A Avenue
Surrey, BC V3S 2A7
www.rmbooks.com

Rocky Mountain Books
PO Box 468
Custer, WA
98240-0468

Library and Archives Canada Cataloguing in Publication

Jennings, Neil L
Coastal beauty : wildflowers and flowering shrubs of coastal British
Columbia and Vancouver Island / Neil L. Jennings.
Includes index.

ISBN 978-1-897522-02-8

1. Wild flowers–British Columbia–Pacific Coast–Identification.
2. Flowering shrubs–British Columbia–Pacific Coast–Identification.
3. Wild flowers–British Columbia–Vancouver Island–Identification.
4. Flowering shrubs–British Columbia–Vancouver Island–Identification.
I. Title.

QK203.B7J463 2008   582.1309711'1   C2007-907288-7

Library of Congress Control Number: 2007943346

Edited by Joe Wilderson
Proofread by Corina Skavberg
Interior design by John Luckhurst
All cover and interior photos supplied by Neil L. Jennings except as
otherwise noted

Printed and bound in Hong Kong

Rocky Mountain Books gratefully acknowledges the financial support of the
Government of Canada through the Book Publishing Industry Development
Program (BPIDP); the Canada Council for the Arts; and the province of British
Columbia through the British Columbia Arts Council and the Book Publishing
Tax Credit for our publishing activities.

This book has been produced on 100% post-consumer recycled paper,
processed chlorine free and printed with vegetable-based dyes.

ACKNOWLEDGEMENTS

When I commenced work on this book, I was aware that I would need assistance in obtaining photographs of many of the included species. In that regard I contacted a number of wildflower photographers who were known to me, and some who were perfect strangers. Their generous support was heartening, and, indeed, without it the project could not have been completed in the timeframe desired. Heartfelt thanks go to the photographers who generously and graciously permitted me to use some of their work in the book: Roman Stone of Cobble Hill, British Columbia; Kevin Newell of Victoria, British Columbia; Dave Ingram of Courtenay, British Columbia; Tracy Utting of Iqaluit, Nunavut; Gill Ross of Okotoks, Alberta; and Jim Riley of Randle, Washington. Particular thanks also go to Virginia and Doug Skilton of Surrey, British Columbia, who not only generously contributed photographs but were also extraordinarily forthcoming with advice and assistance on the completion of the book. I also want to thank Jim and Anne Williams, Susan Leacock, and Brian Saunders, all of Victoria, British Columbia, for their tremendous kindness and hospitality extended on my field trips to gather photographs for the book. I also want to tip my hat to Rose Klinkenberg, who administers E-Flora BC (www.eflora.bc.ca), which website provided me with a tremendous amount of research information, and Genevieve Singleton of Duncan, British Columbia, who is the warden for the Honeymoon Bay Ecological Reserve. Lastly, I want to thank my wife, Linda, for her support, encouragement, patience, and companionship in our past and future outings.

*This book is dedicated to the memory of Bruce McKinnon –
beloved husband, son, brother, artist, a man for all seasons –
a good man in a storm. Too soon gone; sorely missed; fondly
remembered.*

CONTENTS

INTRODUCTION

This book is intended to be a field guide for the amateur naturalist to the identification of wild flowering plants commonly found in the coastal area of the Pacific Northwest. This is not a book for scientists. It is a book for the curious traveller who wants to become acquainted with the flowers encountered during outings. This book differs from most other field guides in that it has large, clear photographs of the species treated; it makes no assumption that the reader has a background in things botanical – as seems to be assumed in many other guides; and it is small enough to actually carry in the field and not be a burden. I believe that most people want to be able to identify the flowers they encounter because that ability enriches their outdoor experience. Some might think it a difficult skill to perfect, but take heart and consider this: you can easily put names and faces together for several hundred family members, friends, acquaintances, movie stars, authors, business and world leaders, sports figures, etc. Wildflower recognition is not different from that, and it need not be complicated.

For purposes of this book, the area of interest is loosely defined as coastal British Columbia (including Vancouver Island), Washington, and Oregon, from coastal elevations eastward and upward to the alpine community on the western side of the coastal mountains. Plants do not recognize man-made boundaries, and overlap occurs. The floral community on the eastern slopes of the coastal mountains and the dry plateaus and arid basins of the interiors of British Columbia, Washington, and Oregon are not addressed, owing to the limitations of space available in the book. Indeed, this book would virtually double in size – and weight – if that floral community were included. A companion book, *Central Beauty: Wildflowers and Flowering Shrubs of the Southern Interior of British Columbia,* also published by Rocky Mountain Books, addresses those species.

This book does not cover all of the species of wildflowers and flowering shrubs that exist in the Pacific Northwest, but it does cover a large representation of the floral community that might be encountered in a typical day during the blooming season. No book that I am acquainted with covers all species in the region, and indeed if such a book existed, it would be a tome that could not be easily carried. For example, it is estimated that in the Composite Family (Sunflowers) alone there are over 1,000 species in over 100 genera in the area. Obviously, space will not permit a discussion of all such species, nor would it be pertinent for the amateur naturalist. The region harbours a vast diversity of habitat. Indeed, for its relative size, the region is said to have the greatest diversity of plant species of any comparable area in North America. In fact, it is probably fair to say that the area contains more floral diversity than virtually any comparable area on the planet, outside of tropical environments.

"Do you know what this flower is called?" is one of the most often asked questions when I meet people in the field. Hopefully, this book will enable the user to answer the question. Identification of the unknown species is based on comparison of the unknown plant with the photographs contained in the book, augmented by the narrative descriptions associated with the species pictured. In many cases the exact species will be apparent, while in other cases the reader will be led to plants that are similar to the unknown plant, thus providing a starting point for further investigation. I believe that most people will have a richer experience outdoors if they learn to recognize the wildflowers they encounter. For the purposes of this book, scientific jargon has been kept to a minimum. I have set out to produce the best photographic representations I could obtain, together with some information about the plant that the reader might find interesting and that might assist the reader in remembering the names of the plants. What I am attempting to do is assist people who want to be able to recognize and identify common wildflowers they see while outdoors. I have tried to keep it simple, while making it interesting and enjoyable. In my view, what most people really want to know about wildflowers is "what is this thing?" and "tell me something interesting about it." Botanical detail, while interesting and enlightening to some of us, will turn off many people.

The plants depicted in the book are arranged first by colour and then by family. This is a logical arrangement for the non-botanist because the first thing a person notes about a flower is its colour. All of the plants shown in the book are identified by their prevailing common names. Where I knew of other common names applied to any plant, I noted them. I have also included the scientific names of the plants. This inclusion is made to promote specificity. Common names vary significantly from one geographic area to another; scientific names do not. If you want to learn the scientific names of the plants to promote precision, fine. If you do not want to deal with that, fine. Just be mindful that many plants have different common names applied to them depending on geography and local usage.

A few cautionary comments and suggestions:

While you are outdoors, go carefully among the plants so as not to damage or disturb them. In parks, stay on the established trails. In large measure, those trails exist to allow us to view the natural environment without trampling it to death. Many environments are delicate and can be significantly damaged by indiscriminately tromping around in the flora.

Do not pick the flowers. Leave them for others to enjoy. Bear in mind that in national, provincial, and state parks it is illegal to pick *any* flowers.

Do not attempt to transplant wild plants. Such attempts are most often doomed to failure, and such practices can have devastating consequences for wild stocks.

Do not eat any plants or plant parts. To do so presents a potentially significant health hazard. Many of the plants are poisonous – some violently so.

Do not attempt to use any plants or plant parts for medicinal purposes. To do so presents a potentially significant health hazard. Many of the plants are poisonous – some violently so.

One final cautionary note: the pursuit of wildflowers can be addictive, though not hazardous to your health.

Neil L. Jennings
Calgary, Alberta

PLANT SHAPES AND FORMS

Parts of a Leaf

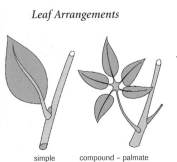

vein
midrib
blade
petiole
node

Parts of a Flower

stamen { filament, anther
petal
stigma
style
ovary } pistil
sepal
receptacle
pedicel

Leaf Arrangements

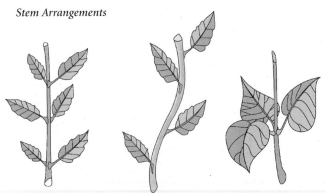

simple   compound – palmate   compound – pinnate   compound – doubly pinnate

Stem Arrangements

opposite   alternate   whorled

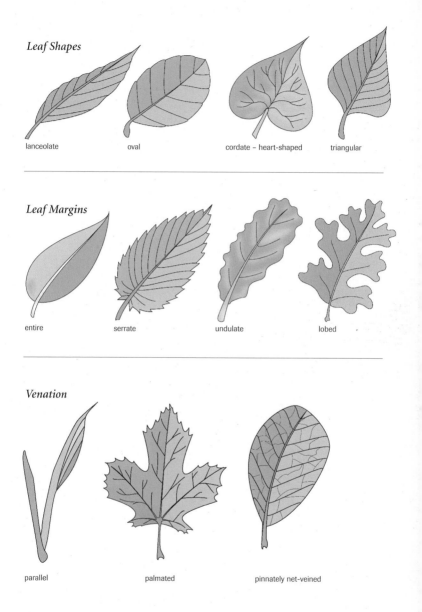

Leaf Shapes

lanceolate   oval   cordate – heart-shaped   triangular

Leaf Margins

entire   serrate   undulate   lobed

Venation

parallel   palmated   pinnately net-veined

TERRITORIAL RANGE OF WILDFLOWERS

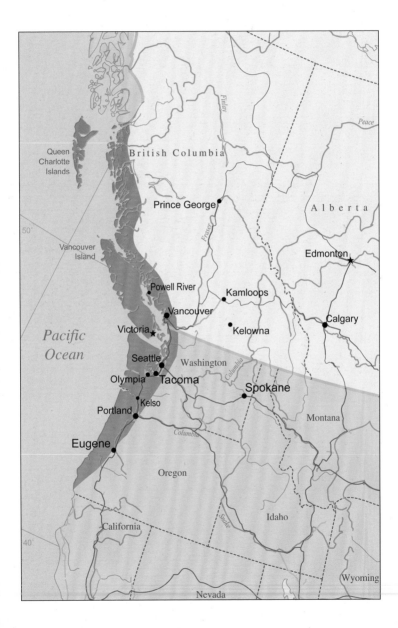

Red, Orange, and Pink Flowers

This section contains flowers that are red, orange, or pink when encountered in the field. Flowers that are pinkish often can have tones running to lavender, so if you do not find the flower you are looking for, check the other sections of this book.

Wild Ginger
Asarum caudatum

BIRTHWORT FAMILY

This plant is a low, creeping, matted perennial that appears in moist, shady woods at low to middle elevations. The plant is easily missed owing to its low-growing habit. The paired, opposite, glossy, evergreen leaves are kidney- to heart-shaped, 4–10 cm long and slightly wider, and are borne on long, hairy stalks. The flower nestles between the leaves, often hidden by them. The flower is purple-brown, solitary, and has three distinctive, long (3–8 cm), tapering petals. The plant exudes a faint odour of ginger, and is pollinated by flies, ants, millipedes, and other "creepy crawlers."

The genus name, *Asarum*, is derived from the Greek *asaron*, an Old World species. The species name, *caudatum*, is Latin for "tailed," a reference to the long, tapering petals on the flower. Native peoples used the plant for a variety of medicinal purposes. A tea was brewed from the root to treat colds, indigestion, and stomach pains, and the leaves were used in poultices applied to boils, skin infections, and toothaches. The plant is not related to the gingers used in Asian cuisine, which are in the genus *Zingiber*.

Falsebox
Paxistima myrsinites (formerly *Pachistima myrsinites*)

BITTERSWEET FAMILY

This dense evergreen shrub grows low to the ground or up to 60 cm tall at low to middle elevations in coniferous forests. The branches on the plant are reddish brown and exhibit four ridges. The leaves are opposite, glossy, leathery, and sharply toothed. The relatively inconspicuous flowers are tiny, brick red to maroon, cruciform-shaped with four petals, occurring in clusters along the branches in the leaf axils. The flowers bloom early in the year and are quite fragrant.

The genus name, *Paxistima*, is derived from the Greek *pachus*, meaning "thick," and *stigma*, a reference to the thick stigmas of the flowers on the plant. The species name, *myrsinites*, is derived from the Greek word for myrrh, the gum resin used in perfumes, medicine, and incense. This reference is undoubtedly to the fragrance of the flowers. The common name of the plant is derived from the Latin *buxus*, a "box" being a receptacle that was made from the boxwood tree, a tree that is reminiscent in form and foliage to this plant. The plant is also known as Mountain Boxwood, Oregon Boxwood, and Mountain-Lover. The branches from the plant are used extensively in the florist trade, even to the point of depleting the native stocks in places.

Water Smartweed (Water Knotweed)
Polygonum amphibium

BUCKWHEAT FAMILY

This plant occurs from prairie to subalpine elevations, and is found in ponds, marshes, ditches, and lakeshores, often forming mats in standing water. The plant may grow on land adjacent to or in the water. The leaves are large, oblong to lance-shaped, rounded or pointed at the tips, and have a prominent midvein. The flowers are pink and occur in a dense, oblong cluster at the top of thick, smooth stalks.

The genus name, *Polygonum*, is derived from the Greek *poly*, meaning "many," and *gonu*, meaning "knee." The authorities differ on whether this refers to the contorted, many-jointed rootstock from which the plant grows, or to the numerous joints in the stems of the plants in this genus. The contorted shape of the rhizome is probably the source of the common name for many plants in the genus – Knotweed. The species name, *amphibium*, refers to the aquatic habitat of the plant. The plant was used by Native peoples both medicinally – in poultices to treat piles and skin disease – and as food. The plant is also food for a large variety of birds.

Red Columbine (Western Columbine)
Aquilegia formosa

BUTTERCUP FAMILY

These beautiful flowers are found in meadows and dry to moist woods, and are among the showiest of all western wildflowers. The leaves of the plant are mostly basal and compound, with three sets of three leaflets each. The flowers occur on stems above the basal leaves, and the stem leaves are smaller than the basal leaves, only appearing with three leaflets each. The five petals have red spurs above, and yellow blades below. The five sepals are red. Numerous stamens extend well beyond the petal blades.

The origin of the genus name, *Aquilegia*, is the subject of some debate. One school holds that it is from the Latin *aquila*, meaning "eagle," and is a reference to the long, talon-like spur on the flower. Another school argues that the genus name is from *aqua*, meaning "water," and *legere*, meaning "collect," a reference to the drops of nectar that gather at the ends of the spurs. The common name, Columbine, is derived from *columba*, meaning "dove," it being said that the petals resembled a group of doves drinking at a dish. An interesting juxtaposition, with the war symbol eagle in one camp, and the peace symbol dove in the other. The species name, *formosa*, means "comely" or "beautiful." The plant also goes by the locally common names of Western Columbine and Sitka Columbine. Bumblebees and butterflies favour Columbines. Where the range of this plant and Yellow Columbine (*A. flavescens*) overlap, they may hybridize to produce flowers with pink-tinged sepals.

Western Meadow Rue
Thalictrum occidentale

BUTTERCUP FAMILY

Western Meadow Rue is a dioecious species, which means that the male and female flowers are found on separate plants. The leaves on the plant are very similar in appearance to those of Columbines (*Aquilegia*), occurring in threes, but this plant's leaves are three times ternate – 3 x 3 x 3 – for a total of 27 leaflets per leaf. Neither gender of flowers has any petals. The male flower resembles a small wind chime, with the stamens hanging down like tassels. The female flowers resemble small star-shaped pinwheels. The plant prefers cool, moist forest environments.

The genus name, *Thalictrum*, is derived from the Greek *thallos*, which means "young shoot" or "green bough," a reference to the plant's bright green early shoots. The species name, *occidentale*, means "of the West." Native peoples used the plant variously as a medicine, a love charm, and a stimulant to horses. In modern times the plant is being investigated in chemotherapy research for cancer for its naturally occurring bioagents.

Bull Thistle
Cirsium vulgare

COMPOSITE FAMILY

This plant is a Eurasian weed that was introduced to North America and is common in pastures, waste places, clearings, and roadsides. The flowers are large composite heads with purple disk flowers and no ray flowers. The flower heads are bulbous and covered in sharp spikes. The flower structure is extraordinarily intricate when examined closely. The leaves, both basal and stem, are lance-shaped, deeply lobed, and spiny, clasping the stem. The Bull Thistle will grow to over 2 m tall, and will produce a multitude of flowers.

There is some dispute among the authorities as to the origin of the genus name, *Cirsium*. One school argues that the name originates from the Greek *kirsos*, which means "swollen vein," a condition that these plants were once said to heal. The other school opines that the genus name is derived from the Latin *circum*, which means "around," possibly a reference to the fact that many members of the genus have spikes on the entire rounded surface of the flower heads. All thistles have spines on their leaf edges, but the Bull Thistle is the only one with a spiny leaf surface. The flowers are a favourite of bees and butterflies. The thistle generally is the national emblem of Scotland, legend having it that a soldier in an invading Danish army stepped on a thistle and cried out in pain, awaking and alerting the Scottish encampment, who rose and repelled the invading army. The thistle was thereafter considered to be the guardian of Scotland. Bull Thistle is also known locally as Spear Thistle.

Canada Thistle
Cirsium arvense

COMPOSITE FAMILY

Despite the common name, this noxious weed was introduced to North America from Eurasia. The plant grows to over 1 m tall from a thin, white, creeping rhizome. The flowers occur in heads at the tops of the multiple branches. The flowers are usually pinkish to mauve, but they may be white. The leaves are alternate and oblong to lance-shaped, with wavy margins.

The origin of the genus name, *Cirsium*, is explained in the narrative on Bull Thistle (*C. vulgare*), on page 7. The species name, *arvense*, means "of cultivated fields," and the plant certainly lives up to its name. By combining a creeping rhizome and tremendous seed distribution, the plant will quickly take over areas where it grows. If the rhizome is cut or broken by farm machinery, the spread of the plant is exacerbated. Canada Thistle is dioecious – that is, male and female flowers occur on separate plants.

Orange Agoseris (Orange-Flowered False Dandelion)
Agoseris aurantiaca

COMPOSITE FAMILY

This is a common plant in moist to dry openings, meadows, and dry open forests in mid to alpine elevations. The plant is also known as False Dandelion, and occurs in both yellow (*A. glauca*) and orange. Agoseris shares many characteristics with the Dandelion (*Taraxacum officinale*), shown on page 234, including a long taproot, a rosette of basal leaves, a leafless stem, a single flower appearing on a long stalk, and the production of a sticky, milky juice that is apparent when the stem is broken. Agoseris is generally a taller plant than Dandelion, its leaves are longer, and the leaf blades are smooth or faintly toothed rather than deeply incised as Dandelion's are. The bracts of the Agoseris flower heads are broader than Dandelion, and are never turned back along the stem as they are in Dandelion.

The genus name, *Agoseris*, is the Greek name for an allied Old World plant. The species name, *aurantiaca*, means "orange." Some Native peoples used the milky juice of the plant as a chewing gum. Infusions from the plant were also used for a variety of medicinal purposes.

Orange Hawkweed
Hieracium aurantiacum

COMPOSITE FAMILY

A plant common to open woods, meadows, roadsides, ditches, and disturbed areas from low to subalpine areas, this conspicuous flower is an introduced species from Europe, where it has long been a garden ornamental. The species can spread rapidly and become a noxious weed. Indeed, one common name applied to the plant is Orange-Red King Devil. The orange flower heads appear in a cluster on ascending stalks. The flowers are composed entirely of ray florets; there are no disk florets. The leaves are broadly lance- to spoon-shaped, in a basal rosette.

The genus name, *Hieracium*, is derived from the Greek *hierax*, which means "hawk," as it was once believed that eating these plants improved a hawk's vision. The species name, *aurantiacum*, means "orange coloured." The leaves, stems, and roots produce a milky latex that was used as a chewing gum by British Columbia tribes. A white form of Hawkweed (*H. albiflorum*), shown on page 90, also appears in the region in open woods, but its white flowers appear singly at the tops of many-branched stems, not as clusters.

Pink Pussytoes
Antennaria rosea

COMPOSITE FAMILY

This mat-forming species is a low perennial that spreads by trailing stems, and occurs from valley floors to the subalpine zone. The leaves are spatula-shaped, and grey-hairy on both surfaces. The basal leaves are larger than those on the slender stem of the plant. The flower heads are composed entirely of disk florets that are pinkish. The flower heads are surrounded by several thin, translucent, overlapping bracts.

In the *Antennaria* genus, the male and female flowers are on separate plants. The genus name is derived from the Latin *antenna*, the reference being that the male flowers have parts that resemble the antennae of an insect. The soft, fuzzy flower heads of this genus give it the common name – Pussytoes – and a number of species occur in the same general habitat. The species name, *rosea*, refers to the colour of the flower heads.

Black Gooseberry (Swamp Currant)
Ribes lacustre

CURRANT FAMILY

This is an erect deciduous shrub, growing up to 1.5 m tall, that occurs in moist woods and open areas from foothills to the subalpine zone. The branches of the plant have small prickles and stout thorns at leaf and branch bases. The leaves are alternate and shaped like maple leaves, with three to five deeply cleft, palmate lobes. The flowers are reddish, saucer-shaped, and hang in elongated clusters. The fruits are dark purple to black berries, which bristle with tiny hairs.

The genus name, *Ribes*, is derived from the Arabic *ribas*, the Moorish medical name for an unrelated rhubarb-like plant that grows in North Africa and Spain. The species name, *lacustre*, is derived from the Latin *lacus*, meaning "lake," or *lacustris*, meaning "inhabiting lakes." The genus includes all of the Currants and Gooseberries. This plant is also known as Bristly Black Currant and Black Swamp Gooseberry. Commonly, members of the *Ribes* genus are divided into Currants and Gooseberries depending upon whether or not the berries are bristly hairy – Currants are not bristly hairy, and Gooseberries are. The spines on the plant can cause allergic reactions in some people.

Flowering Red Currant (Red-Flower Currant)
Ribes sanguineum

CURRANT FAMILY

This early-blooming plant is an upright shrub that grows to 3 m tall in open, dry woods, along roadsides, and in logged areas from low to middle elevations. It has reddish-brown bark, and the leaves are triangular, deeply three-lobed, toothed and up to 6 cm wide. The flowers are numerous, rose-red to pink, tubular with five spreading lobes, and occur in clusters, with 10–20 flowers blooming together. The unpalatable fruit is round, black and often covered with a blue bloom.

The origin of the genus name, *Ribes*, is discussed in the note on Black Gooseberry (*R. lacustre*), shown on page 12. All of the currants and gooseberries are in this genus. The species name, *sanguineum*, means "blood red," a reference to the inflorescence of the plant. This plant has been used extensively as a garden ornamental. Indeed, in 1827 the redoubtable explorer and plant collector David Douglas (namesake of the Douglas fir) carried seeds for Flowering Red Currant back to England and sold them, making sufficient funds on the sale to recover the entire cost of his just-ended two-year expedition. Red-Flowering Gooseberry, also known as Gummy Gooseberry (*Ribes lobbii*), also appears in the area. Its flowers are also reddish, but they resemble fuchsias in shape, often occurring in pairs.

Spreading Dogbane
Apocynum androsaemifolium

DOGBANE FAMILY

A fairly common shrub in thickets and wooded areas, this plant has freely branching, slender stems. The leaves are opposite, egg-shaped, and have sharp-pointed tips. The leaves generally droop during the heat of the day. The small, bell-shaped, pink flowers droop from the ends of the leafy stems, usually in clusters. The petal lobes are spreading and bent back, usually with dark pink veins.

The genus name, *Apocynum*, is derived from the Greek *apo*, meaning "against," and *kyon*, meaning "dogs," thus the common name. The pods of the plant are poisonous and it may have been that the pods were used to concoct a poison for dispensing with unwanted dogs. The tough fibres from the stems of Dogbanes were rolled into a strong, fine thread by Native peoples. Several strands plaited together were used for bow strings, and the cord was also used to make fishing nets. When broken, the leaves and stems exude a milky sap. The plant contains a chemical related to the heart disease drug called digitalis, and was once used as a digitalis substitute, but harmful side effects brought an end to that practice. A similar species, Indian-Hemp Dogbane (*A. cannabinum*) occurs in similar habitat, but it is a generally larger species with small flowers and ascending leaves. The two species can overlap and interbreed, producing an intermediate species known as Western Dogbane.

Fireweed (Great Willowherb)
Epilobium angustifolium

EVENING PRIMROSE FAMILY

A plant of disturbed areas, roadsides, clearings, and shaded woods that occurs from low elevations to the subalpine zone. This plant is often one of the first plants to appear after a fire. The pink, four-petalled flowers bloom in long terminal clusters. Bracts between the petals are narrow. The flowers bloom from the bottom of the cluster first, then upward on the stem. The leaves are alternate and appear whorled.

The genus name, *Epilobium*, is derived from the Greek *epi*, meaning "upon," and *lobos*, meaning "a pod," a reference to the inflorescence of plants of this genus occurring on top of the seed pod. The species name, *angustifolium*, means "narrow-leafed." The common name originates from the plant's tendency to spring up from seeds and rhizomes on burned-over lands. The leaves resemble willow leaves, hence the alternative common name Willowherb. The young leaves can be used in salads, and a weak tea can be brewed from the plant. The inner pith can be used to thicken soups and stews. Fireweed is the floral emblem of the Yukon.

River Beauty (Broad-Leaved Willowherb)
Epilobium latifolium

EVENING PRIMROSE FAMILY

Also known as Dwarf Fireweed, this plant grows as a pioneer, often in dense colonies, on gravelly floodplains, and river bars, where the dense leaves and waving pink to purple flowers often obscure the stony ground underneath. River Beauty strongly resembles common Fireweed (*E. angustifolium*), shown on page 15, in appearance, but it has much shorter stems, broader leaves, and larger, more brilliantly coloured flowers. The large and showy, pink to rose-purple, four-petalled flowers bloom in a loose, short, leafy inflorescence. The leaves are bluish-green and waxy, with rounded tips.

The origin of the genus name, *Epilobium*, is explained in the narrative on Fireweed. The species name, *latifolium*, means "broad-leaved." Plants in this genus are also known by the locally common name of Willowherb. This plant is also locally known as Broad-Leaved Willowherb and Mountain Fireweed. The plant is cooling and astringent, and was used by some Native peoples to promote healing of wounds. Another related species, Alpine Willowherb (*E. anagallidifolium*) occurs in the area. That species is a low, mat-forming plant that appears in moist to wet rocky areas in the subalpine and alpine zones. The flowers are tiny, and may be pink to rose-coloured to white.

Foxglove
Digitalis purpurea

FIGWORT FAMILY

This European import is an erect, unbranched biennial or short-lived perennial that grows up to 2 m tall in disturbed open ground, at forest edges and along roadsides. The leaves are alternate, hairy, ovate to lance-shaped, coarsely toothed and up to 40 cm long at the base, diminishing in length as they move up the flowering stem. A number of pink to purple flowers appear in a one-sided raceme along the erect stem. The individual flowers have a corolla that is up to 6 cm long. They are five-lobed, with the lower three lobes fused into a longer, hairy, prominent lip, and the upper two lobes fused into a shorter lip. There are dark purple spots inside the lower lip.

The genus name, *Digitalis*, is derived from the Latin *digitus*, which means "finger," a reference to the flower shape, which will allow a finger to be inserted. The species name means "purple." The leaves, flowers, and seeds of the plant contain the cardiac glycoside digitoxin, which is fatal if ingested. The compound is referred to clinically as digitalis and is used to treat heart failure. The common name Foxglove is said to have come from Old English *foxes glofa*, which pertains to an old myth that held that foxes used the flowers to sheath their paws and thereby allowed them to make stealthy nocturnal raids on chicken coops.

Red Monkeyflower (Lewis' Monkeyflower)
Mimulus lewisii

FIGWORT FAMILY

This plant occurs, often in large patches, along mountain streams, and other moist areas in the subalpine and alpine zones. The leaves are clasping, opposite, conspicuously veined, and have irregular teeth along the margins. The showy red flowers arise from the axils of the upper leaves. The corolla is funnel-shaped and has two lips. The upper lip is two-lobed and often bent backward, and the lower lip is three-lobed, with hairs in the throat and yellow markings on the lobes.

The origin of the genus name, *Mimulus*, is discussed in the note on Yellow Monkeyflower (*M. guttatus*), shown on page 252. The species name, *lewisii*, is in honour of Meriwether Lewis of the Lewis and Clark Expedition, who collected the first specimen of the plant in 1805 near the headwaters of the Missouri River in what is now the State of Montana. Hummingbirds and bees are attracted to these flowers.

Red Paintbrush
Castilleja miniata

FIGWORT FAMILY

A plant of alpine meadows, well-drained slopes, open subalpine forests, moist stream banks, and open foothills woods, Paintbrush is widely distributed and extremely variable in colour. The leaves are narrow and sharp-pointed, linear to lance-shaped, usually without teeth or divisions, but sometimes the upper leaves have three shallow lobes. The showy red, leafy bracts, which are actually modified leaves, resemble a brush dipped in paint, hence the common name.

The genus name, *Castilleja*, commemorates Domingo Castillejo, an 18th-century Spanish botanist. The species name, *miniata*, refers to the scarlet-red colour minium, an oxide of lead. There are a number of species of Paintbrush in the region and they vary enormously in colour – from pink, to red, to yellow, to white – but their general appearance is distinctive and recognizable, regardless of colour. Some of the colour variations are shown on the next page. Specific identification is outside the ambit of this volume, and if you wish more specific identifications I encourage consultation with other authorities. Although beautiful, this plant should not be transplanted as it is partially parasitic and does not survive transplanting.

Paintbrush Colour Variations

Virginia Skilton images

Western Corydalis (Scouler's Corydalis)
Corydalis scouleri

FUMITORY FAMILY

Jim Riley image

This is an erect, thinly branching plant with soft, hollow stems that grows to 120 cm tall in wet, shady, forest openings and woodlands at various elevations. The leaves are large, three-times pinnately divided, with thin, delicate leaflets. The flowers are purplish, with a long, pink spur, and they occur in a raceme at the top of the stems. The fruits are pod-like capsules that burst explosively when ripe, spreading seeds over considerable distances.

The genus name, *Corydalis*, is derived from the Greek *korydallis*, which means "crested lark," a reference to the spur of the petal resembling the spur of a lark. The species name, *scouleri*, honours Dr. John Scouler, who accompanied David Douglas on some of his explorations in the Pacific Northwest region in 1825. Another member of the genus, Golden Corydalis (*C. aurea*), is a common plant east of the coastal mountains. It is a smaller plant overall, and has yellow flowers. Corydalis are generally considered poisonous because they contain isoquinoline and other alkaloids. Some poisoning of livestock has been reported.

Wild Bleeding Heart
Dicentra formosa

FUMITORY FAMILY

This plant grows from spreading rhizomes in moist, shady woods, along steams, and in dry open areas at low to middle elevations, often forming clumps. The plant has fern-like foliage. The flowers are pink, up to 2.5 cm wide, and occur in a panicle of 2 to 20 flowers above the leaves on leafless flowering stalks that reach 40 cm tall. The flowers are distinctively heart-shaped, with colouring that resembles a drop of blood descending from the heart.

The genus name, *Dicentra*, is derived from the Greek *dis*, which means "twice," and *kentron*, which means "spur," a reference to the two outer petals of the flower resembling spurs. The species name, *formosa*, means "beautiful," or "comely." This plant also goes by the locally common names of Pacific Bleeding Heart and Western Bleeding Heart. Bleeding Heart has long been used as a garden ornamental, and a number of cultivars have been developed, producing flowers of a wide variety of colours.

Dove's-Foot Crane's-Bill
Geranium molle

GERANIUM FAMILY

Kevin Newell image

This plant is a spreading, hairy annual that puts up a flowering stem 40 cm tall in moist disturbed ground. It is a native of Europe, but is well naturalized in most of North America. The plant is covered with soft, white hairs. The basal leaves are round, with five to nine deep lobes, and form a rosette on the ground. The stem leaves are similar but smaller. The flowers are pink to purplish, have five lobes with notched tips, and have deeper coloured pencilling inside the petals. The flowers also exhibit hairiness, and they usually occur in pairs on the stem. The fruits are elongated and said to resemble a crane's bill.

The genus name, *Geranium*, is derived from the Greek *geranos*, meaning "crane," the reference being that the fruits are shaped like a crane's bill. The species name, *molle*, means "soft," a reference to the hairs on the plant. Northern Geranium (*G. erianthum*) also exists in the region. It has blue-purple flowers with dark purple penciling on the petals. Two other similar European invaders inhabit the region: Herb Robert (*G. robertianum*), shown on page 24; and Stork's-Bill (*Erodium cicutarium*), which has fern-like leaves and small magenta-coloured flowers. Interestingly, *Erodium* is Greek for heron, another different long-legged, long-beaked avian. Geraniums can get confusing with all the bird references to cranes, herons, storks, and now doves.

23

Herb Robert
Geranium robertianum

GERANIUM FAMILY

This plant is a Eurasian import that is looked upon as a noxious weed in North America. It is usually confined to low elevations but is very adaptable and may be found up to mid-montane elevations. It has decumbent to ascending stems that are branched, spreading, hairy and up to 60 cm tall. The leaves are mostly on the stem and they are pinnately divided into three to five segments, then again deeply cleft, giving them a fern-like appearance. Freshly picked leaves exude a pungent, musky odour when crushed, giving rise to another common name, Stinky Bob. The leaves turn to brilliant red and bronze colours in the fall and in times of drought. The five-petalled flowers are pink to reddish-purple with white pencilling, hairy, 1 cm in diameter, rounded at the tips and occur, usually in pairs, at the top of the stems and in the leaf axils.

The origin of the genus name, *Geranium*, is discussed in the note on Dove's-Foot Crane's-Bill (*G. molle*), shown on page 23. The origin of the species and common names is the subject of much debate and disagreement. Some say it is named for St. Robert of Molesme, an 11th-century healer, because the flower blooms around his Saint's Day, April 29. Others say the name is derived from European folklore. In England it is said to be named for Robin Hood. In Germany it is associated with the Hob Goblin – Knecht Rupert or Black Peter – the dark side of St. Nicholas. The plant has long been used in traditional herbalism to treat a variety of conditions from nosebleed to toothache to dysentery. The plant is also said to have an antiseptic and styptic effect and has been used to treat wounds.

Bearberry (Kinnikinnick)
Arctostaphylos uva-ursi

HEATH FAMILY

This trailing or matted evergreen shrub grows low to the ground, and has long branches with reddish, flaky bark and leathery, shiny green leaves. The flowers are pale pink and urn-shaped, appearing in clumps at the ends of the stems. The fruits are dull red berries.

The genus name, *Arctostaphylos*, is derived from the Greek *arktos*, meaning "bear," and *staphyle*, meaning "bunch of grapes." The species name, *uva-ursi*, is Latin for "bear's grape." The berries are apparently relished by bears and birds, though they tend to be dry and mealy to humans. They are edible and have been used as food, prepared in a variety of ways. The berries remain on the plant through the winter. One of the common names, Kinnikinnick, is believed to be of Algonquin origin, and means "something to smoke," a reference to the fact that some Native peoples used the leaves of the plant as a tobacco.

Black Huckleberry(Thinleaf Huckleberry)
Vaccinium membranaceum

HEATH FAMILY

This erect, densely branched, deciduous shrub grows up to 1.5 m tall at mid- to high elevations in dry to moist coniferous forests. The leaves are lance-shaped to elliptic, with pointed tips and finely toothed margins. The leaves turn red or purple in the fall. The flowers are creamy pink and urn-shaped, nodding on slender stalks. The fruits are black to dark purple berries, 8–10 mm across.

Without question, the berry of this plant is among the most sought-after wild berries that occur in the mountains – by human consumers, birds and bears. The sweet taste of the berry is distinctive, and the berries are used to make jams, syrups and liqueurs. Among those who harvest the berries, picking sites are jealously guarded. My son once asked a picker where he found the berries. The picker answered: "Sonny, I would sooner tell you I was sleeping with your wife than I would where I pick Huckleberries!" A similar species, Red Huckleberry (*V. parvifolium*), occurs in the region, but it has pinkish-yellow flowers and produces a bright red berry.

Bog Cranberry
Vaccinium oxycoccos (also *Oxycoccus oxycoccus*)

HEATH FAMILY

This plant is a creeping, vine-like, dwarf evergreen shrub that grows up to 40 cm tall in bogs and in wet sphagnum moss, from low to subalpine elevations. The stems are thin, wiry and slightly hairy. The small leaves are alternate, leathery, sharp-pointed, and widely spaced on the stem. The leaves are dark green on the upper surface, lighter underneath, and the margins curl under. The nodding flowers are deep pink, with four petals that curve backward exposing the stamens, reminiscent of the shape of Broad-Leaved Shooting Star (*Dodecatheon hendersonii*), shown on page 217. The fruits are round red berries that appear disproportionately large for the tiny stems on which they hang.

The genus name, *Vaccinium*, is the Latin name for Blueberry. The species name, *oxycoccos*, is derived from the Greek *oxys*, meaning "acid, sharp or bitter," and *kokkos*, meaning "round berry," a reference to the tart taste of the fruits. The berries are rich in vitamin C, and were used by Native peoples as a food. Another so-called Cranberry appears in the area – the Low-Bush Cranberry (*Viburnum edule*), shown on page 110 – but it is a member of the Honeysuckle Family, and is a substantially different plant. Another plant found in areas east of this region, Lingonberry (*V. vitis-idaea*), is also commonly known as Bog Cranberry, but it has larger, leathery leaves, and white to pinkish urn-shaped flowers.

Candy-Stick
Allotropa virgata

HEATH FAMILY

Roman Stone image

This unusual plant grows up to 50 cm tall in deep humus of coniferous forests at low to moderate elevations. It resembles a peppermint stick, with maroon or red and white striping up the stem. Young plants resemble asparagus, with a slight pinkish tint or no colour at all. As the plant matures it becomes red and white striped. The flowers are numerous, white with red centres, and are distributed along the stem in the axils of the "leaves." There are no true "leaves," just white, scaly bracts. As the plant dies, it turns to brown, and may stand in place for up to three years.

The genus name, *Allotropa*, is derived from the Greek *allos*, which means "different," or "other," and *trope*, which means "turning," possibly a reference to the young flowers facing upward and the older ones downward. The species name, *virgata*, is Latin and means "striped." This is the only member of the genus. Like a number of others in the Heath Family, this plant is saprophytic, meaning it cannot produce chlorophyll, and gains its nourishment from decaying organic matter in the soil. Not surprisingly, the plant goes by the locally common names of Sugarstick and Barber's Pole.

Copperbush
Elliottia pyroliflorus (formerly *Cladothamnus pyroliflorus*)

HEATH FAMILY

Virginia Skilton image

This flowering shrub grows up to 2 m tall in cool, shady, subalpine forests and along stream banks. The stems are erect, and the bark is loose, shredding, and copper-coloured. The leaves are pale green, smooth, somewhat waxy, alternate, imperfectly whorled on the stem, and have an abrupt tooth-like tip. The copper-coloured flowers are solitary, five-petalled, saucer-shaped up to 4 cm across, and borne on the ends of the branches. The distinctive thing about the flower, apart from its colour, is the long, curved, protruding style.

The genus name, *Elliottia*, honours 19th-century American banker, legislator, and botanist Stephen Elliott. The species name, *pyroliflorus*, means "leaves like Pyrola," a reference to the flowers on this plant resembling those of *Pyrola*, the Wintergreens, with the protruding style.

False Azalea (Fool's Huckleberry)
Menziesia ferruginea

HEATH FAMILY

This deciduous shrub is erect and spreading, and grows up to 2 m tall in moist, wooded sites in the foothills to subalpine zones. The twigs of the shrub have fine, rust-coloured, sticky, glandular hairs, and give off a skunky odour when crushed. The leaves are alternate, elliptic, and broader above the middle. They are grey-hairy and have a prominent midvein protruding at the tip. The flowers are small, pinkish to greenish-orange, urn-shaped, and nodding on long, slender stalks. The flowers occur in clusters at the base of new growth. The fruit is a dark purplish capsule.

The genus name, *Menziesia*, honours Archibald Menzies, a physician and botanist who accompanied Captain George Vancouver in his northwest explorations in the late 18th century. The species name, *ferruginea*, is Latin meaning "iron rust," a reference to the rusty glands that cover the branches and the leaves. In the fall the leaves of the shrub take on very attractive orange and crimson colours. The common name False Azalea arises because the leaves of this plant resemble those of garden Azaleas. Another common name for the plant is Fool's Huckleberry, because the flowers might be mistaken for those of Huckleberries.

Gnome Plant
Hemitomes congestum

HEATH FAMILY

Jim Riley image

This rare plant lives in the rich humus in damp coniferous forests at middle elevations in the mountains. The emerging plant resembles a small cauliflower head. It has no leaves, only white, scaly bracts. The flower is small and pink, with four petals fused together into a tubular corolla 12–20 mm long. Five to 20 individual flowers are congested at the tip of the stem, resembling, in some people's estimation, a sponge.

The genus name, *Hemitomes*, is derived from the Greek *hemi*, meaning "half," and *tomias*, meaning "sterile" or "eunuch," a reference to the sterility of one anther. The species name, *congestus*, means "arranged very closely," or "very crowded," a reference to the congestion of flowers at the top of the stem. This plant is a saprophyte, deriving its nourishment from decaying organic matter in the soil where it grows. The plant also goes by the locally common name of Coneplant, though, considering its overall rarity, it may be oxymoronic to refer to anything about this plant as common.

Grouseberry
Vaccinium scoparium

HEATH FAMILY

This low deciduous shrub grows up to 20 cm tall and often forms dense ground cover on slopes in the foothills to subalpine zone. The branches are numerous, slender and erect. The leaves are alternate, ovate, widest in the middle and sharp-pointed, with finely serrated margins. The flowers are small, pinkish, urn-shaped and nodding, hanging down singly from the leaf axils. The fruits are tiny, edible, bright red berries.

The Grouseberry is a member of the same genus as Blueberries, Huckleberries, and Cranberries. The species name, *scoparium*, is derived from the Latin *scopula*, meaning "broom-twig," a reference to the close, twiggy stems on the plant. The berries are very small, and some Native peoples gathered them using combs. Small mammals and birds eat the berries. Grouse eat all parts of the shrub, thus the common name Grouseberry. An allied species, Dwarf Blueberry (*V. caespitosum*), appears in similar habitat. It is a matting plant with reddish twigs, and it also has five-lobed bell-shaped flowers that are borne singly from the leaf axils. Its fruits are small, blue, edible berries. Grouseberry is also known as Grouse Whortleberry. Whortleberry is a name applied in Europe to Bilberry, an Old World Blueberry.

Oval-Leaved Blueberry
Vaccinium ovalifolium

HEATH FAMILY

This deciduous shrub grows to over 2 m tall in moist to wet coniferous forests, clearings, and bogs at low to subalpine elevations. The pale pink flowers are urn-shaped, and appear singly at the leaf bases. The flowers may precede the arrival of the leaves. The berries are blue-black, dusted with a pale bluish bloom. The berries are somewhat large for wild blueberries, and have a pleasant flavour. The leaves are oval, blunt, and rounded at the ends, and usually lack teeth on the margins.

The genus *Vaccinium* includes all of the wild Blueberries, Cranberries, and Huckleberries. The species name, *ovalifolium*, refers to the shape of the leaves. Another common name applied to this plant is Blue Huckleberry.

Pine-Drops
Pterospora andromedea

HEATH FAMILY

This purple or reddish-brown saprophyte (a plant that gets its nutrients from decaying plant or animal matter) stands up to a metre tall or more, and lives in deep humus of coniferous or mixed woods. The plants grow singly or in clusters, but they are rare. The leaves are mostly basal, and resemble scales. The stem stands erect, and is covered with glandular hairs. The flowers are cream-coloured to yellowish, and occur in a raceme that covers roughly the top half of the stalk. The petals are united into an urn shape, and hang downward off bent flower stalks, like small lanterns. The stalks of the plant will remain erect for a year or more after the plant dies.

The genus name, *Pterospora*, is derived from the Greek *pteron*, meaning "wing," and *sporos*, meaning "seed," a reference to the winged appearance of the seeds. The species name, *andromedea*, refers to Andromeda of Greek mythology. To review the story of Andromeda, see White Heather (*Cassiope mertensiana*), shown on page 108. I am at a complete loss as to how the taxonomist connected this plant to that particular myth, and I have so far been unable to explain the connection.

Pink Rhododendron
Rhododendron macrophyllum

HEATH FAMILY

A compact, rounded evergreen shrub that grows to 6 m tall in coniferous forests and open thickets at low elevations in the region. The leaves are oblong-elliptic, leathery, up to 20 cm long, glossy and shiny on top, and appear in whorls around the branches. The flowers are pink, five-lobed with the petals fused, and they appear in clusters at the ends of branches. The flowers have spotting in the throat, with protruding anthers that are covered with fleshy hairs.

The origin of the genus name, *Rhododendron*, is discussed in the note on White Rhododendron (*R. albiflorum*), shown on page 109. The species name, *macrophyllum*, refers to the large leaves of the species. This plant is the floral emblem of the State of Washington. All parts of the plant contain poisonous alkaloids that are toxic to humans and livestock. This plant also goes by the locally common names of Pacific Rhododendron and California Rhododendron.

Pink Wintergreen

Pyrola asarifolia

HEATH FAMILY

This plant is an erect perennial that inhabits moist to dry coniferous and mixed forests, and riverine environments, from the montane to the subalpine zone. The flowers are shaped like an inverted cup or bell, nodding, waxy, pale pink to purplish red, and have a long, curved, projecting style. The leaves are basal in a rosette. The leaves have a leathery appearance, and are shiny, rounded, and dark green.

The origin of the genus name, *Pyrola*, is explained in the narrative on Greenish-Flowered Wintergreen (*P. chlorantha*), shown on page 99. The species name, *asarifolia*, is derived from the Latin *asarum*, meaning "ginger," and *folium*, meaning "leaf," a reference to the similarity between the leaves of this plant and those of wild ginger. Members of the genus contain salicylic acid, a compound very like the active ingredient in aspirin. In fact, the compound was originally isolated from the bark of willows, which are in the genus *Salix*. Two other species of *Pyrola*, Greenish Flowered Wintergreen and One-Sided Wintergreen (*P. secunda*), shown on page 104, occur in similar habitat.

Pipsissewa (Prince's-Pine)
Chimaphila umbellata

HEATH FAMILY

This small evergreen shrub grows to 30 cm tall in coniferous woods. The dark green, glossy leaves are narrowly spoon-shaped, saw-toothed, and occur in whorls. The flowers are pink, waxy, saucer-shaped, and nodding on an erect stem above the leaves. The fruits of the plant are dry, round, brown capsules that often overwinter on the stem.

The genus name, *Chimaphila*, is derived from the Greek *cheima*, meaning "winter," and *philos*, meaning "loving," descriptive of the evergreen leaves. Pipsissewa is an adaptation of the Cree name for the plant, *pipsisikweu*, meaning "it breaks into small pieces," a reference to a substance in the leaves that was said to dissolve kidney and gall stones. The plant was often used to make a medicinal tea. Both Native peoples and settlers to North America used the plant for a variety of medicinal purposes. A related species, Menzies' Pipsissewa or Little Prince's Pine (*C. menziesii*), shown on page 103, occurs in the area, but it is a much smaller plant and has white flowers.

Red Heather (Pink Mountain Heather)
Phyllodoce empetriformis

HEATH FAMILY

This dwarf evergreen shrub grows up to 30 cm tall, and thrives in subalpine and alpine meadows and slopes near timberline. The leaves are blunt, needle-like, and grooved on both sides. The red to pink, urn-shaped flowers are erect and/or nodding in clusters at the top of the stems.

The genus name, *Phyllodoce*, appears to honour a sea nymph from Greek mythology, but none of the learned authorities seem to know why that mythical character is associated with this genus. The species name, *empetriformis*, also is a source of controversy. Some authorities say the name arises because the leaves of this plant resemble those of the genus *Empetrum* – the Crowberry Family. Other authorities say the species name is derived from the Greek *en*, meaning "on," and *petros*, meaning "rocks," a reference to the rocky habitat favoured by the plant. This plant is not a true heather, but it has been called by that name for so long that it might as well be. The first sample of the plant was collected by Lewis and Clark during their expedition, but the exact location of its collection has been lost.

Salal

Gaultheria shallon

HEATH FAMILY

Dave Ingram image

This evergreen plant is a sprawling shrub that grows up to 3 m tall and forms dense, impenetrable thickets in openings and coniferous forests from the coast to low mountain elevations. The leaves are thick, leathery, sharply toothed at the tip, generally elliptic, but rounded at the base. The flowers are pink, urn-shaped, nodding, hairy, 7–10 mm long, and occur in clusters (racemes) at the branch tips. The fruits are edible blue-black berries.

The genus name, *Gaultheria*, honours Dr. Jean-François Gaultier, an 18th-century French-Canadian physician and naturalist. Native peoples called the plant Salal, and the species name, *shallon*, is the Latinized version of that name. Native peoples made extensive use of the fruits as food, drying them and forming them into flat cakes. Foliage from the plant is often used in the florist trade. An allied species, Western Tea-Berry (*G. ovatifolia*), shown on page 107, occurs in the same range, but is a low, ground-covering plant.

Swamp Laurel (Western Bog Laurel)
Kalmia microphylla

HEATH FAMILY

This low-growing evergreen shrub occurs in cool bogs, on stream banks, and lakeshores in the subalpine and alpine zones. The leaves are leathery, dark green above and greyish-white beneath, often with the margins rolled under. The flowers are pink to rose-coloured, with the petals fused together to form a saucer or bowl, appearing on a reddish stalk. There are 10 purple-tipped stamens protruding from the petals.

The genus name, *Kalmia*, is to honour Peter Kalm, a student of Carolus Linnaeus at Uppsala University in Sweden. Linnaeus was a prominent botanist who developed binomial nomenclature for plants. The species name, *microphylla*, means "small-leaved." The leaves and flowers of this plant contain poisonous alkaloids that can be fatal to humans and livestock if ingested.

Orange Honeysuckle (Western Trumpet)
Lonicera ciliosa

HONEYSUCKLE FAMILY

This is a climbing vine up to 6 m long that clambers over trees and shrubs in woodlands and forest openings from low to high elevations. It seems to prefer to climb on conifers. The leaves are broadly elliptic, up to 10 cm long, opposite on the stem, except the uppermost pair, which are connate – fused at their bases to form a shallow cup – and hairy on the margins. The flowers are vividly orange, tubular, up to 4 cm long, and appear in clusters of 5 to 25 blooms from inside the connate leaves. Unlike many members of the genus, these flowers have no scent.

The origin of the genus name, *Lonicera*, is discussed in the note on Black Twinberry (*L. involucrata*), shown on page 256. The species name, *ciliosa*, refers to the hairs on the margins of the connate leaves. This plant is also known by the locally common name Western Trumpet. Hairy Honeysuckle (*L. hispidula*), shown on page 199, is a related species that appears in similar habitat. It has a cluster of wine-purple flowers in its connate leaves. Native peoples used the stems of honeysuckles to fashion woven mats, bags, baskets, and blankets.

Snowberry
Symphoricarpos albus

HONEYSUCKLE FAMILY

This common deciduous shrub occurs from coast to coast in North America, and is found from prairies to lower subalpine zones, in well-drained, open or wooded sites. There are several subspecies that are so alike it requires dissection and magnification to tell one from the other. The shrub is erect, and grows up to 2 m tall. The branches are opposite and slender, and on close examination are seen to be covered with tiny hairs. The leaves are opposite, elliptic to oval, and pale green. The flowers are pink to white, and broadly funnel-shaped, occurring in clusters at the ends of the twigs. The stamens and style do not protrude from the flower. The fruits are waxy, white berry-like drupes that occur in clusters, and often persist through the winter.

The genus name, *Symphoricarpos*, is derived from the Greek *symphorein*, which means "borne together," and *karpos*, which means "fruit," a reference to the clustered berries of the plant. The berries of this plant were not eaten by Native peoples, and many considered them poisonous. In fact, some Natives called the berries Corpse Berries and Ghost Berries. Some Native peoples believed that these white berries were the ghosts of Saskatoon berries, and thus part of the spirit world and not to be tampered with by the living.

Twinflower
Linnaea borealis

HONEYSUCKLE FAMILY

This small, trailing evergreen is common in coniferous forests, but easily overlooked by the casual observer. This plant sends runners creeping over the forest floor, over mosses, fallen logs, and stumps. At frequent intervals the runners give rise to the distinctive Y-shaped stems, 5–10 cm tall. Each fork of the stem supports at its end a slightly flared, pink to white, trumpet-like flower that hangs down like a small lantern on a tiny lamppost. The flowers have a sweet perfume that is most evident near evening.

The genus name, *Linnaea*, honours Carolus Linnaeus, the Swedish botanist who is the father of modern plant nomenclature. It is said that this flower was his favourite among the thousands of plants he knew. The species name, *borealis*, means "northern," referring to the circumpolar northern habitat of the plant. Some Native peoples made a tea from the leaves of this plant.

Columbia Lily (Tiger Lily)
Lilium columbianum

LILY FAMILY

True lilies are recognized by their large, showy flowers, smooth, unbranched stems, and whorls of narrow, lance-shaped leaves. Columbia Lily can have up to 30 flowers per stem. The orange to orange-yellow flowers are downward-hanging, with curled-back petals and deep red to purplish spots near the centre. The flowers are very similar to Western Wood Lily (*L. philadelphicum*), the floral emblem of the Province of Saskatchewan, but the Wood Lily petals form more of a chalice shape, without the petals curling back like those of this species.

The common name, Tiger Lily, most probably comes from the spotting on the petals. There was once a superstition that smelling this species would give you freckles. The bulbs of the plants were used as food by Native tribes. They were said to have a peppery taste, and would add a peppery taste to other foods. Like many other lilies, this one will die if the flower is picked. The bulb depends upon the flower for nutrients, and if the flower is removed, the bulb will starve and die.

Hooker's Onion
Allium acuminatum

LILY FAMILY

This plant grows from an ovoid, checkerboard-patterned corm in dry, rocky areas and grasslands. The corm puts up an erect, stout, leafless, flowering stem that is up to 30 cm tall. There are two to three basal leaves that are linear and almost as tall as the flowering stem, but they wither prior to blooming. The inflorescence is an open umbel of 10 to 20 stalked flowers, each rose pink in colour, bell-shaped, and having six distinct tepals. The tepals are spreading and somewhat reflexed at their pointed tips. The plant often forms extensive patches.

The origin of the genus name, *Allium*, is explained in the note on Nodding Onion (*A. cernuum*), shown on page 46. The species name, *acuminatum*, is derived from the Latin *acuminate*, which means "pointed," a reference to the pointed tips on the tepals of the flower. Hooker in the common name refers to Joseph Dalton Hooker, 19th-century director of the Royal Botanic Gardens in England, considered by many to be the most important botanist of that century. This plant also goes by the locally common name Tapertip Onion.

Nodding Onion
Allium cernuum

LILY FAMILY

All *Allium* species smell strongly of onion, and have small flower clusters at the top of the leafless stalk. Nodding Onion is a common species in the region, and is easily identified by its pink drooping or nodding inflorescence. There are usually 8–12 flowers in the nodding cluster.

The stem gives off an oniony odour when crushed, and is said to be one of the better tasting wild onions. Native peoples gathered the bulbs and ate them raw and cooked; used them for flavouring other foods; and dried them for later use. Ground squirrels also use this plant in their diets. *Allium* is the Latin name for "garlic," said to be from the Celtic *all*, meaning "hot" or "burning," because it irritates the eyes. The species name, *cernuum*, refers to the crook in the stem of the plant just below the flower.

Pink Fawn Lily
Erythronium revolutum

LILY FAMILY

This early-blooming lily favours moist, open woods, forest edges, and stream banks, usually in sandy humus at lower elevations. The plant has two large (10–20 cm) dark green, elliptic basal leaves that are very attractively mottled with brown or white. The lovely pink flower appears at the top of a leafless, smooth stem, usually as a solitary, but an individual plant may have as many as three flowers. The flowers are nodding, with six reflexed tepals that often display yellow bands at the base of the inner surface.

The genus name, *Erythronium*, is derived from the Greek *erythrus*, meaning "red," a reference to a similar Old World species (*E. dens-canis*), which has pink to reddish flowers, and was said to produce a red dye. Pink Fawn Lilies are often found in large clumps. The plant has a number of locally common names, including Trout Lily, Dog's Tooth Violet, and Mahogany Fawn Lily. White Fawn Lily (*E. oregonum*), shown on page 127, is a very similar species that occurs in similar habitat. Another member of the genus, Glacier Lily (*E. grandiflorum*), shown on page 257, occurs at higher elevations.

Musk Mallow
Malva moschata

MALLOW FAMILY

Jim Riley image

This sparsely hairy perennial is a native of Europe that has naturalized in North America. It grows from a taproot, producing ascending, branched stems up to 60 cm tall in disturbed ground and along roadsides. The basal leaves are heart- to kidney-shaped, 8 cm long, hairy, and toothed to shallowly lobed. The stem leaves are rounded, five-lobed to the base, and dissected into fine linear segments. The flowers appear in clusters at the top of the stems. Each flower is white to pink, and has five spreading petals.

The genus name, *Malva*, is the Latin name for Mallow. Mallow is derived from the Greek *malache* or *malakos*, a reference to an ornament made from the seeds which was supposed to be soothing to the skin. The species name, *moschata*, means "having a musty scent." Hollyhocks are in the same genus.

Hedge-Nettle
Stachys cooleyae (also *S. chamissonis*)

MINT FAMILY

This plant inhabits wetland marshes, moist woods, banks and shores of streams and lakes, and swampy low ground. The plant has a single stem that is square in cross-section, bristly, and stands up to 120 cm tall. The leaves are wedge to egg-shaped, coarsely toothed, hairy on both surfaces, 10 cm long, and occur in opposite pairs on the stem. The red-purple flowers occur in whorled, interrupted clusters in the axils of the leaves on the upper stem. The individual flowers are tubular, up to 4 cm long, and have two lips. The upper lip is two-lobed, erect, and usually shorter than the three-lobed lower lip.

The genus name, *Stachys*, is derived from Greek and means "spike" or "ear of corn," a reference to the inflorescence type. The specific name honours Grace Emily Cooley, a 19th-century American botanist and professor. *Chamissonis* is a synonymous specific name that honours 19th-century French-born German botanist Adelbert von Chamisso, who worked in California and accompanied a Russian expedition in search of the Northwest Passage. This plant also goes by the locally common name Staggerweed.

Fairy Slipper (Venus Slipper)
Calypso bulbosa

ORCHID FAMILY

This is an orchid found in shaded, moist coniferous forests. The flowers are solitary and nodding on leafless stems. The flower has pinkish to purplish sepals, and mauve side petals. The lip is whitish or purplish, with red to purple spots or stripes, and is hairy yellow inside. The flower is on the top of a single stalk, with a deeply wrinkled appearance. This small but extraordinarily beautiful flower blooms in the early spring, often occurring in colonies.

The Fairy Slipper has many common names, including Venus Slipper and Calypso Orchid. The genus name, *Calypso*, is derived from Greek mythology, Calypso being a daughter of Atlas. *Calypso* means "concealment," and is very apt, given that this flower is very easy to miss, being small, delicate, and growing in out-of-the-way places. The species name, *bulbosa*, refers to the bulb-like corm from which the flower grows. Do not attempt to transplant this flower. It needs specific fungi in the soil to grow successfully. Its range has diminished over time, owing to over-picking.

Spotted Coralroot (Summer Coralroot)
Corallorhiza maculata

ORCHID FAMILY

A plant of moist woods and bogs, this orchid grows from extensive coral-like rhizomes. There are no leaves, but the plant has several membranous bracts that sheath the purplish to brownish stem. A number of flowers appear on each stem, loosely arranged up the stem in a raceme. The three sepals and two upper petals are reddish purple. The lip petal is white, with dark red or purple spots and two lateral lobes.

The origin of the genus name, *Corallorhiza*, is explained in the narrative on Striped Coralroot (*C. striata*), shown on page 52. Lacking chlorophyll, this plant does not produce food by photosynthesis, but rather through parasitizing fungi in the soil. Several other Coralroots occur in the same habitat as the Spotted. Western Coralroot (*C. mertensiana*) is yellowish below, unspotted, and has a lip that is generally reddish-purple or white with two purple blotches.

Striped Coralroot
Corallorhiza striata

ORCHID FAMILY

A plant of moist woods and bogs, this orchid grows from extensive coral-like rhizomes, and occurs in the montane and subalpine zones. The pink to yellowish-pink flowers have purplish stripes on the sepals, and the lowest petal forms a tongue-shaped lip. A number of flowers appear on each stem, loosely arranged up the stem in an unbranched raceme. The leaves are tubular sheaths that surround, and somewhat conceal, the base of the purplish stem.

The genus name, *Corallorhiza*, is derived from the Greek *korallion*, meaning "coral," and *rhiza*, meaning "root," a reference to the coral-shaped rhizomes from which the plant grows. The species name, *striata*, refers to the striped markings on the flower. Of the coralroots, the Striped Coralroot has the largest flowers. Striped Coralroot is sometimes referred to as Madder-Stripes or Hooded Coralroot. Spotted Coralroot (*C. maculata*), shown on page 51, occurs in the same habitat. The coralroots depend on a complex relationship with fungi in the soil for germination and survival.

Beach Pea
Lathyrus japonicus (also *L. maritina*)

PEA FAMILY

This plant grows from a rhizome and spreads up to 1.5 m, trailing and climbing over other plants on sandy beaches and coastlines around the northern hemisphere. The thick and sturdy rhizome anchors the plant firmly in place in the sand. The leaves are compound with 6 to 12 elliptic, leathery leaflets on sturdy stems, and tendrils at the leaf tips. The flowers are reddish-purple to bluish, pea-like, and occur in a loose, stalked cluster of two to eight flowers from the leaf axils. The fruits are in pods that resemble those of garden peas.

The genus name, *Lathyrus*, is from the Greek *lathyros*, an old name for "pea." The specific name, *japonicus*, means "of or belonging to Japan," which is most probably a reference to the far-flung habitat of the plant. The seeds of the plant remain viable for up to five years while floating in seawater, allowing quite sufficient time for the plant to go from Japan to North America. The leaves of the plant are used in Chinese traditional medicine.

Perennial Pea
Lathyrus latifolius

PEA FAMILY

This plant is a European native that was introduced as a garden ornamental and has escaped from the garden to establish itself in disturbed ground, along roadsides and railway lines, and in other low-elevation environments. The plant arises from sprawling rhizomes and can grow to 1.5 m tall. The leaves are compound, but with only two elliptic leaflets that are up to 14 cm long and appear opposite each other on the stem. Each leaf has long, many-branched tendrils at the leaf tip which allow the plant to climb over other vegetation. The pea-like flowers are 2 cm long, reddish-pink, and occur in clusters of up to 15 flowers on upright stems.

The origin of the genus name, *Lathyrus*, is explained in the note on Beach Pea (*L. japonicus*), shown on page 53. The species name, *latifolius*, means "broad-leaved," and this plant is also known as Broad-Leaved Peavine. Though this plant is somewhat invasive, it has been beneficial in some areas because its extensive root system can help to stabilize soil and prevent erosion on steep banks.

Red Clover
Trifolium pratense

PEA FAMILY

A European species now well established in North America, Red Clover grows to 60 cm tall in low to middle elevations. The leaves are in threes, often displaying a white crescent-shaped spot near the base. The flowers are pea-like, pinkish to purple, and up to 200 of them occur in a dense head, 2–3 cm in diameter, at stem tops. Two leaves lie immediately below the flower head.

All clovers have leaves in threes and flowers in dense heads. The name Clover is derived from the Latin *clava*, meaning "club," and more particularly the triple-headed cudgel carried by Hercules. That club bears a resemblance to the shape of the leaf on Clover. The suit of clubs in cards is from the same root, and has the same shape. White Clover (*T. repens*), shown on page 140, is a similar plant in the same habitat. White Clover has a creeping stem and white to pinkish flowers on longer stalks. Herbalists favour Red Clover in the treatment of skin problems.

Thrift (Sea-Pink)
Armeria maritima

PLUMBAGO FAMILY

Virginia Skilton image

This plant is a grass-like perennial that grows on beaches and coastal bluffs. The narrow leaves are mainly in a basal clump and look like grass, with one to several leafless flowering stems rising above the basal leaves to 50 cm tall. The inflorescence is a compact, crowded globe of pink to lavender flowers that have been likened to pom-poms. The individual flowers are tubular with five petals. The whole inflorescence is cupped in brown, papery bracts.

The genus name, *Armeria*, is Latinized from the Old French name *armoires*, which was the name for a different cluster-headed flower in the Pink Family. The species name, *maritima*, is a reference to the sea coast habitat of the plant. The common name, Thrift, is probably an acknowledgement that the plant would have to exhibit some thriftiness if it is to survive in the rather harsh habitat where it lives.

Scarlet Pimpernel
Anagallis arvensis

PRIMROSE FAMILY

This European import is a sprawling plant, with decumbent to ascending stems that may reach 40 cm long. Garden escapees have naturalized in lowland fields and waste areas in the region. The leaves are egg-shaped, on the stem only, unstalked, somewhat clasping, and opposite in pairs. Each pair is set at right angles to the next pair along the stem. The salmon pink to red flowers are solitary in the leaf axils, on curved stalks up to 4 cm long. The flowers are 5–10 mm wide, five-lobed, with the lobes divided almost to the bases and fringed with fine hairs. The fruits are spherical capsules that break open for seed dispersal.

The authorities cite two origins for the genus name, *Anagallis*. Some say the name is derived from the Greek *anagaleo*, which means "to make happy." Others say that the origin is from the Greek *ana*, which means "again," and *agallein*, which means "to delight in." Whichever is accurate, there seems to be agreement that the reference is that these attractive flowers close when the sun is obscured, and reopen when the sun returns. This habit of the plant gives rise to the locally common name Poor Man's Weather Glass. The species name, *arvensis*, means "of cultivated fields."

Dwarf Raspberry (Arctic Blackberry)
Rubus arcticus (also *R. acaulis*)

ROSE FAMILY

This plant is a low, creeping, dwarf shrub that grows from a trailing rootstock, and is most often found in wet meadows and around seeps in the subalpine and alpine zones. The leaves are divided into three leaflets that are round to heart-shaped, and have coarsely toothed edges. The flowers are usually solitary, pink, and five-petalled. The fruits are clusters of red to purple drupelets, the aggregate of which is the raspberry. The fruits are small, but sweet and flavourful.

The genus name, *Rubus*, is the Latin name for brambles, from the root *rubra*, meaning "red," a reference to the colour of the fruits of many members of the genus. The berries have long been used as food, and some Native peoples used them to concoct a tea. The plant is also locally known as Dwarf Nagoonberry, but the origin of that name is unclear. One possible origin for that name is the Tlingit people of southern Alaska, where the plant is common. In the Tlingit language the fruit of this plant is called *neigoon*, which may have been anglicized to nagoon.

Dwarf Woodland Rose (Baldhip Rose)
Rosa gymnocarpa

ROSE FAMILY

This is a slender, straggly shrub that grows to over 1 m tall in moist to dry woods and forest areas in the region. Its leaves are pinnately compound with five to nine elliptic, double-toothed leaflets that are 4 cm long. The plant is armed with numerous slender thorns. The flowers are the familiar pink wild roses, borne singly on short stems from the leaf axils, with golden stamens in the centre of the spreading pink petals. The fruits are round, red, shiny rosehips that have no withered sepals attached.

The genus name requires no explanation. The species name, *gymnocarpa*, means "naked fruit," a reference to the rosehips that have no withered sepals attached. This is the only member of the genus that does not retain the withered sepals on the ripe fruits. Rosehips are high in vitamin C and are a favourite food of many species of birds. They can also be used to make a wonderfully flavourful jelly. Native peoples used rose plants for medicinal purposes, and made fishing lures from the thorns.

Hardhack (Douglas' Spirea)
Spiraea douglasii

ROSE FAMILY

This is an erect, deciduous, freely branching shrub that forms dense, impenetrable thickets up to 2 m tall in marshy areas and along streams in low to middle elevations. The leaves are oblong, elliptic, 3–9 cm long, and notched at the tips. The inflorescence is a tall, elongated cluster of hundreds of tiny pink flowers. The flowers are relatively short-lived, quickly turning brown and drab in appearance.

The genus name, *Spiraea*, is from the Greek *speira*, which means "twisted," or "wound together," possibly a reference to plants of this genus being used as garlands. The species name honours the intrepid Scottish explorer and botanist David Douglas. The common name, Hardhack, is said to arise because the dense thickets of the plant are hard to hack through for hikers, loggers and any others who might try to move through an area where they grow. Ungulates browse the plants, and butterflies and bees are drawn to the flowers. The plant also has the locally common name of Steeplebush. Subalpine Spirea (*S. densiflora*), also called Pink Spirea by some, is a similar plant that occurs in subalpine areas in the region. It too has pink flowers, but they occur in a dense, flat-topped or rounded cluster.

Nootka Rose
Rosa nutkana

ROSE FAMILY

This is a medium-sized shrub that grows up to 3 m tall in open habitats at low to middle elevations. The plant is armed with a pair of large prickles near the bases of the leaves. The leaves are alternate, deciduous, pinnately compound with five to seven egg-shaped to elliptic, saw-toothed leaflets with rounded tips. The flowers are large, typical of wild roses, and usually occur singly at the ends of the branches. The fruits are round, purplish-red rosehips that have the withered sepals attached as a beard.

The specific name, *nutkana*, refers to Nootka Sound in British Columbia, where the plant was first collected for science. Portions of the plant were used by Native peoples to flavour foods. The branches and bark of the plant were used to concoct a tea, and that concoction was also used by some tribes for medicinal purposes such as eyewash, poultices for sore eyes, and treating any type of abscess.

Salmonberry
Rubus spectabilis

ROSE FAMILY

This perennial, early-blooming bush grows up to 4 m tall from rhizomes in moist woods and along streams at low to montane elevations. The stems are arching, have shredding bark, and are armed with numerous short, straight, prickles. The leaves are trifoliate, with pointed leaflets and coarsely double-toothed margins. The flowers are showy, with five reddish-pink spreading petals, and occur singly or in small groups at the ends of the stems. The fruit is a large, red, sweet, soft, edible berry that is up to 2.5 cm long.

The origin of the genus name, *Rubus*, is explained in the note on Dwarf Raspberry (*R. arcticus*), shown on page 58. The specific name, *spectabilis*, means "showy," a reference to the flowers, which are one of the few in the genus that are other than white. The common name, Salmonberry, originated with Native peoples along the Columbia River. The fruits have long been used as food.

Roseroot
Sedum integrifolium

STONECROP FAMILY

This plant occurs in the subalpine and alpine zones, favouring moist rocky scree, talus, and ridges. The stems arise from a fleshy rootstock, and they are covered in persistent leaves. The leaves are oval to oblong, fleshy, and somewhat flattened. The flowers have oblong petals, are rose-coloured to purple, and occur in rounded, flat-topped, dense clusters atop the stems.

The origin of the genus name, *Sedum*, is discussed in the note on Lance-Leaved Stonecrop (*S. lanceolatum*), shown on page 268. The species name, *integrifolia*, indicates that the leaf margins are entire and not cut or toothed. When the roots are cut or bruised, they give off the fragrance of roses, thus the common name. Another common name is King's Crown, a reference to the shape of the inflorescence. Some Native peoples used Roseroot medicinally in poultices.

Sea Blush (Rosy Plectritis)
Plectritis congesta

VALERIAN FAMILY

This slender upright annual grows up to 60 cm tall in moist meadows, on open slopes, and on rocky bluffs, sometimes blooming in such profusion that the hillsides and fields take on a pink hue. The erect stems are usually angled and somewhat square in cross-section. The basal leaves have short stalks, but usually disappear prior to blooming. The stem leaves are few and widely spaced on the stem, opposite, oblong, stalkless, and have smooth margins. The inflorescence occurs at the top of the stem in a dense, head-like cluster of numerous small, pink flowers. Individual flowers are five-lobed, with two lobes vertical and three lobes widely flared.

The genus name, *Plectritis*, is derived from the Greek *plektron*, which means "pleated," a reference to the densely complex inflorescence. The specific name means "congested," also a reference to the ball of flowers.

White, Green, and Brown Flowers

This section includes flowers that are predominantly white or cream-coloured, green, or brown when encountered in the field. Given that some flowers fade to other colours as they age, if you do not find the flower you are looking for in this section, check the other sections in the book

Vanilla Leaf
Achlys triphylla

BARBERRY FAMILY

This plant spreads by rhizomes, and will carpet the understorey in shady, moist sites in deep woods, open parkland, and forest edges. The large leaves are divided into three leaflets, similar to huge clover leaves, with scalloped margins that appear winged and will nod with even the slightest of breezes. The tiny white flowers appear on an erect stalk that rises above the leaves. The fruits are small, mahogany-coloured seeds that are shaped like a half moon. The plant does not have an aroma when fresh, but the leaves, when dried, emit a distinctive odour of vanilla, hence the common name for the plant.

The genus name, *Achlys*, is derived from Greek and means "thin mist," or "obscurity," a reference to the inconspicuous flowers. The species name refers to the three-parted leaves. Native peoples and early settlers dried the leaves and used them as a repellant for insects, hanging them in lodgings to prevent flies and mosquitoes. Native peoples also used a decoction made from the leaves as a hair wash for lice, as well as a solution to wash floors and furniture to get rid of lice, bedbugs, and other pests. The plant is also known by the locally common names Deerfoot, Sweet-After-Death, and May-Leaf.

Buck-Bean (Bog-Bean)
Menyanthes trifoliata

BUCK-BEAN FAMILY

Jim Riley image

This perennial is an aquatic to semi-aquatic plant that grows up to 30 cm tall from a thick, scaly, creeping rootstock. It appears in swampy land, bogs, ditches, and lake and pond margins. The leaves are basal, clasping, long-stemmed, and compound, with three smooth, elliptical, shiny, green leaflets. The leafless flowering stems arise from the leaves and hold crowded clusters of white flowers at their ends. The flowers are whitish inside, pink to purplish outside, and have a tube-shaped, five-part corolla, densely bearded inside.

The genus name, *Menyanthes*, is said to originate from the Greek *mene*, which means "month," and *anthos*, which means "flower," said to be a reference to the length of time of blooming of the plant. The species name, *trifoliata*, refers to the three-parted leaves. Some Native peoples used the rhizomes of the plant as famine food. They also brewed a tea made from the leaves and used it medicinally for a variety of aliments, including migraine headaches, fevers, and indigestion. The whole plant is also browsed by ungulates. The reference to Bean in the common name is a mystery, this plant bearing no relation whatsoever to beans by way of leaf, flower, or fruit.

Buckbrush (Redstem Ceanothus)
Ceanothus sanguineus

BUCKTHORN FAMILY

Jim Riley image

This erect deciduous shrub grows to 3 m tall in forest openings and edges, in clearings, and in disturbed sites in the montane and subalpine zones. The stems are numerous, erect, smooth, and become purple-red with age. The leaves are alternate, egg-shaped to elliptic, 10 cm long, finely toothed, and hairy on the underside. The fragrant flowers are white, and bloom in dense, fluffy clusters on reddish stems on lateral branches from last year's growth.

The genus name, *Ceanothus*, is derived from the Greek *keanothus*, a name given to an unrelated Old World spiny plant. The specific name, *sanguineus*, means "blood red," a reference to the colour of the stems of the flowering branches. Deer and elk use the plant for winter browse. The leaves and stems of the plant contain a toxic glucoside – saponin – but ungulates seem to suffer no ill effects from eating the plant. It is speculated that the plant has a defensive mechanism to prevent over-browsing by increasing its production of saponin, thus making it unpalatable to the browsers. Early settlers called the plant Soapbloom, the name arising because Native peoples often beat the flowering twigs in water to yield foam. They also used the bark of the plant in poultices for treating burns, and the wood of the plant for fuel. An allied evergreen plant, Snow Brush (*C. velutinus*), shown on page 69, occurs in the same habitat.

Snow Brush (Sticky Laurel)
Ceanothus velutinus

BUCKTHORN FAMILY

This erect evergreen shrub grows to 2 m tall on well-drained slopes in the montane and subalpine forests, and is abundant after a forest fire. The aromatic leaves are alternate and oval, finely toothed, dark green on the top, greyish and smooth underneath. A varnish-like sticky substance covers the upper leaf surface, giving it a shiny appearance and a strong aroma. The leaves have three prominent veins that radiate from the leaf base. The flowers bloom in the early summer, and are tiny and white, heavily scented, and occur in dense clusters on stalks at the ends of the branches.

The origin of the genus name, *Ceanothus*, is explained in the note on Buckbrush (*C. sanguineus*), shown on page 68. Deer and elk often browse on this plant in the winter. The leaves and stems of the plant contain a toxic glucoside – saponin – but ungulates seem to have no ill effects from eating the plant. The seeds of the plant are impervious to moisture and can survive in the forest duff for up to three centuries. The seeds require either heat or scarification to germinate, so young shrubs grow rapidly after a fire, but are eventually shaded out by trees. The locally common name Sticky Laurel arises because of the sticky leaves resembling those of laurel (*Kalmia* ssp.). The plant is also known as Hooker's Ceanothus.

Mountain Sorrel
Oxyria digyna

BUCKWHEAT FAMILY

This relatively low-growing plant often appears in clumps in moist rocky areas, along streams, and at lake margins in the subalpine and alpine zones. The long-stalked leaves are often reddish, primarily basal, smooth with wavy margins, and are distinctively kidney- or heart-shaped. The flowers appear in crowded clusters along several upright stems. The flowers are relatively inconspicuous, tiny, and green to reddish. The fruits are flattened, papery, red seeds that have broad translucent wings.

The genus name, *Oxyria*, is derived from the Greek *oxys*, meaning "sour" or "sharp," a reference to the tart taste of the leaves. The common name, Sorrel, is said to originate from the Old High German word *sur*, meaning "sour." The plant is rich in vitamin C, and is said to be an antiscorbutic – a preventative for scurvy. A number of Native peoples used the plant as food. Mammals and birds also eat the plant.

Sulphur Buckwheat
Eriogonum umbellatum

BUCKWHEAT FAMILY

This perennial grows from a stout taproot and tends to be mat forming. The leaves are all basal. They are spoon- to egg-shaped, narrowing to a slender stalk, greenish above and often woolly white below. The leaves turn bright red in the fall. The flowering stem is usually leafless and up to 30 cm tall. The stem supports an inflorescence composed of small creamy white to pale yellow flowers that are held in compact spherical clusters (umbels). The flowers are sometimes tinged with pink on aging. The plant occurs from moderate to alpine elevations on grassy slopes, dry gravel ridges, alpine ridges, and talus slopes.

The genus name, *Eriogonum*, is derived from the Greek *erion*, which means "wool," and *gonu*, which means "knee" or "joint," a reference to the woolly, jointed stems of many members of the genus. The specific name, *umbellatum*, is a reference to the shape of the inflorescence, and, indeed, this plant also goes by the locally common name Sub-Alpine Umbrellaplant. The flowers of this genus usually have an unpleasant smell, but the nectar appears to be relished by bees, and produces a strongly flavoured, buckwheat-like honey.

Lyall's Anemone (Western Wood Anemone)
Anemone lyallii

BUTTERCUP FAMILY

This plant grows in moist forests and openings from low to subalpine elevations. The stem is erect with three distinctive compound leaves whorled at mid stem. The leaves are on long stems (petioles) and are divided into three lobed leaflets that have rounded, coarse teeth. The flowers are small, white to pink to pale blue, and have only sepals, no petals.

The genus name, *Anemone*, is most probably derived from the Greek *anemo*, meaning "wind," a reference to the fact that the seeds of members of the genus are distributed by the wind. The species name, *lyallii*, honours 19th-century Scottish physician, explorer, naturalist, and naval officer David Lyall. Lyall was in inveterate plant collector who travelled over many parts of the globe. Among his many occupations, he was a member of the Land Boundary Commission that surveyed the border between the United States and British Columbia, and he later wrote the first scientific treatise on the vegetation zones in British Columbia.

Baneberry
Actaea rubra

BUTTERCUP FAMILY

This perennial grows up to 1 m tall in moist shady woods and thickets, along streams, and in clearings from low to subalpine elevations. The plant has one to several stout, upright, branching stems. The leaves are all on the stem. They are divided two or three times into threes, and are coarsely toothed. The inflorescence is a dense, white, cone-shaped cluster of flowers that appears on top of a spike. The fruit is a large cluster of either shiny red or white berries. At the time of flowering, there is no way to determine whether the berries of a particular plant will be red or white.

The common name of the plant is derived from the Anglo-Saxon word *bana*, meaning "murderer" or "destroyer" – undoubtedly a reference to the fact that the leaves, roots and berries of this plant are extremely poisonous. As few as two berries can induce vomiting, bloody diarrhea, and finally, cardiac arrest or respiratory paralysis. The genus name, *Actaea*, is derived from the Greek *aktaia*, meaning "elder tree," as the leaves are similar to elder leaves. The species name, *rubra*, is Latin for "red," a reference to the berries. There have been reports of children who have died as a result of eating the berries.

False Bugbane (Carolina Bugbane)
Trautvetteria caroliniensis

BUTTERCUP FAMILY

This attractive and distinctive perennial grows from a rhizome along stream borders and in moist woods. The leaves are mostly basal, toothed, wider than long, and deeply palmately lobed. The flowers are borne at the terminal ends of an erect, branched stalk that might be as much as 80 cm tall. The white flowers have no petals, only white sepals and many stamens, giving the flower heads the look of round powder puffs.

The genus name, *Trautvetteria*, honours 19th-century Russian botanist E.R. von Trautvetter. The species name, *caroliniensis*, is testament to the plant's wide distribution, as it was first recorded in the Carolinas. The reference to Bugbane in the common name arises from the similarity of this flower to that of Bugbane (*Cimicifuga elata*), which has a distinctively more unpleasant odour. In fact, the genus name *Cimicifuga* is derived from the Latin *cimex*, meaning "bedbug," and *fugo*, meaning "to drive away."

Globeflower
Trollius albiflorus (formerly *T. laxus*)

BUTTERCUP FAMILY

This plant grows from thick rootstock and fibrous roots and is found in moist meadows, along stream banks and in open, damp areas in the subalpine and alpine zones. The mostly basal leaves are shiny, bright green, palmately divided into five to seven parts, and deeply toothed. The stem leaves are few, alternate and short-stalked. The flowers are made up of five to ten white sepals (which may have a pinkish tint on the outside) that surround a central core filled with numerous dark yellow stamens.

There seems to be some confusion among the learned authorities as to the origin of the genus name, *Trollius*. The most likely resolution is that the genus name is a Latinized version of the Swiss-German common name, *trollblume*, which means "troll flower." The reference to the troll, a malevolent supernatural being, probably arises because this plant contains a poisonous alkaloid. Just prior to opening, and during inclement weather, the flower head appears round, thus the common name Globeflower. Globeflower might be confused with Mountain Marsh Marigold (*Caltha leptosepala*), shown on page 76, where they co-exist. The leaves of Mountain Marsh Marigold are heart-shaped, not oblong, and not divided into segments, as are those of Globeflower.

Mountain Marsh Marigold
Caltha leptosepala

BUTTERCUP FAMILY

Virginia Skilton image

This plant lives in marshes, on stream banks, and in seeps in the subalpine and alpine zones. The leaves are mostly basal, simple, long-stemmed, oblong to blunt arrowhead-shaped, with wavy or round-toothed margins. The flowers are solitary on the end of the stem, and consist of 5–12 petal-like sepals that are white, tinged with blue on the back. The flower has a bright yellow centre, composed of numerous stamens and pistils.

The genus name, *Caltha*, is derived from the Greek *kalathos*, which means "goblet," most probably a reference to the shape of the open flower. The species name, *leptosepala*, is derived from the Greek *lepto*, which means "thin or narrow," and *sepala*, referring to the sepals. This plant contains glucosides, which are poisonous. The plant also goes by the locally common names of Elkslip and Elkslip Marshmarigold. Mountain Marsh Marigold might be confused with Globeflower (*Trollius albiflorus*), shown on page 75, which grows in similar habitat. The flowers are similar, but the leaves on Globeflower are deeply divided and sharply toothed.

Western Anemone (Chalice Flower)
Pulsatilla occidentalis (also *Anemone occidentalis*)

BUTTERCUP FAMILY

This plant is considered by many to be characteristic of wet alpine meadows and clearings. The large, creamy-white flowers bloom early in the spring, as the leaves are beginning to emerge. The entire plant is covered with hairs, which keep the plant protected in its cold habitat. Most of the leaves are basal, but there is a ring of feathery, grey-green stem leaves just below the flower. The flower is replaced by a clumped top of plumed seeds at the tip of the flowering stem. These seed clusters have been variously referred to as "mops," "shaggy heads," and "blond wigs," and give rise to another common name, Towhead Babies.

The common name, Chalice Flower, refers to the cup-shape inflorescence of the plant. A more recently coined name that has found some favour is Hippie on a Stick, a reference to the seed pod of the plant. The plant also goes by the locally common name Western Pasqueflower.

Beach Carrot
Glehnia leiocarpa

CARROT FAMILY

Jim Riley image

This ground-hugging perennial plant puts down a deep root system to anchor it in sand on beaches and in coastal dunes adjacent to the ocean. The leaves are basal, thick, leathery, waxy on top and densely white-hairy on bottom, saw-toothed, and pinnately compound, with three leaflets, each split again into three lobes. The flowers are creamy white and occur in an umbel atop short, strong, woolly stems – typical of plants in the carrot family. The fruits are rounded, smooth capsules with wing-like ribs. The fruits are rolled by the wind as a means of dispersal.

The genus name, *Glehnia*, honours 19th-century botanist Peter von Glehn, who was the curator at the St. Petersburg Botanical Garden. The species name, *leiocarpa*, means "smooth seeds," a reference to the rounded fruits of the plant. The plant is also known by the locally common names of American Glehnia and American Silvertop.

Chocolate Tips
Lomatium dissectum

CARROT FAMILY

This large plant has several stout, smooth, hairless stems, and grows to over 1 m tall in dry, rocky places. The leaves are large (up to 30 cm), finely dissected and fern-like, and have a spicy aroma. The surface of the leaves has a covering of fine hairs, making it rough to the touch. The flowers are compound umbels of deep purplish-brown or yellow flowers sitting atop the ends of the stems. The fruits are elliptic seeds with flattened backs and corky, thick-winged margins.

The genus name, *Lomatium*, is derived from the Greek *loma*, meaning "a border," most probably a reference to the winged or ribbed fruit of most of the members of the genus. All members of the genus are edible. The specific name, *dissectum*, describes the finely dissected foliage. Meriwether Lewis collected a specimen of the plant in present-day Idaho in 1806 and labelled it "a great horse medicine among the natives." The plant is also known by the locally common names Fern-Leaved Desert Parsley and Fernleaf Biscuitroot.

Cow Parsnip
Heracleum lanatum

CARROT FAMILY

A plant of shaded riverine habitat, stream banks, and moist open woods, this plant grows to over 2 m tall. The flowers are distinctive in large, compound, umbrella-shaped clusters (umbels) composed of numerous white flowers with white petals in fives. The leaves are compound in threes, usually very large, softly hairy, deeply lobed, and toothed.

Heracleum refers to Hercules, likely because of the plant's large size. Cow Parsnip is also locally known as Indian Celery and Indian Rhubarb. The roots were cooked and eaten by some Native peoples, though there are some sources that say they are poisonous. The Blackfoot roasted the young spring stalks and ate them. They also used the stalks in their Sun Dance ceremony. Caution should be taken to distinguish this plant from the violently poisonous Water Hemlock (*Cicuta maculata*), shown on page 83.

Queen Anne's Lace
Daucus carota

CARROT FAMILY

This is an invasive weed imported from Eurasia, now common in disturbed ground, moist meadows, fields, and roadsides all over North America. It is a single-stemmed biennial that grows to 120 cm tall. The leaves are very finely dissected, like those of garden carrot plants. The inflorescence occurs as compound umbels in compact heads of hundreds of tiny yellow-white aflowers atop the stem. The central floret in the umbel is often purple or pink. When the plant goes to seed, the outer, longer spokes of the umbel arch inward, forming a "bird's nest" effect.

The genus name, *Daucus*, is the Greek name for a similar Old World species. The species name, *carota*, is derived from the Greek *karoton*, which means "carrot." Indeed, this plant is also known as Wild Carrot. There are a number of explanations offered as to the origin of the common name Queen Anne's Lace. As an example, one explanation holds that the name refers to Queen Anne of England, who was an expert lace maker. The legend has it that the Queen, while making lace, pricked her finger with a needle and a drop of blood from the wound fell onto the lace, similar to the purple floret in the middle of the inflorescence.

Sweet Cicely
Osmorhiza berteroi (formerly *O. chilensis)*

CARROT FAMILY

This member of the Carrot Family prefers moist to wet, shady habitat, and grows up to 1 m tall. The leaves are twice divided into three parts, and are deeply cleft and toothed. The flowers are inconspicuous and occur in white to greenish compound, umbrella-shaped clusters. The fruits of the plants in this genus have short beaks that often cling to the fur of passing animals or the clothing of passing hikers.

The genus name, *Osmorhiza*, is derived from the Greek *osme*, meaning "scent," and *rhiza*, meaning "root," a reference to the sweet licorice odour given off by the plant's roots and fruits when they are crushed. Many Native peoples used the roots as food, and also for a variety of medicinal purposes. Some tribes held the plant sacred, and prohibited all but holy men from touching it. The plant is also known locally as Mountain Sweet Cicely.

Water Hemlock
*Cicuta maculata (*also *C. douglasii)*

CARROT FAMILY

This is a plant of marshes, river and stream banks and low, wet areas that produces several large umbrella-like clusters (compound umbels) of white flowers appearing at the top of a sturdy stalk. The leaves are alternate, with many bipinnate and tripinnate leaflets that are lance-shaped. The side veins in the leaflets end between the notched teeth on the leaflets, rather than at their points.

The genus name, *Cicuta*, is the Latin name of some poisonous member of the Carrot Family. While lovely to look at, with its umbrella-shaped clusters of flowers on sturdy stems, the Water Hemlock is considered to be perhaps the most poisonous plant in North America. All parts of the plant are poisonous, as testified to by several common names which include Children's Bane, Beaver Poison, and Death of Man. The toxin – cicutoxin – acts on the central nervous system and causes violent convulsions, followed by paralysis and respiratory failure. Some Native peoples used the powdered root as a poison on arrows. If you touch this plant or cut it with an implement for any reason, wash your hands and the implement immediately and thoroughly.

Daisy Fleabane
Erigeron compositus

COMPOSITE FAMILY

This daisy-like flower is one of several Fleabanes that occur in the region. The leaves of this species are almost all basal, and are deeply divided. The leaves and the flowering stems are sparsely covered with short, glandular hairs. The flowers appear solitary at the top of the stem, and they are typical of flowers in the Composite Family in that they have ray flowers surrounding disk flowers. The ray flowers are numerous, and may be white, pink, or mauve. The disk flowers are numerous and yellow. The involucral bracts are hairy and purplish at the tips.

The genus name, *Erigeron*, is derived from the Greek *eri*, which means "spring," and *geron*, which means "old man," a reference to the hairy-tufted fruits of plants in the genus, or perhaps to the overall hairiness of many species in the genus. The species name, *compositus*, means "well-arranged," probably in reference to the neat appearance of the inflorescence. The common name, Fleabane, arises because it was once thought that bundles of these flowers brought into the house would repel fleas. The plant also goes by the locally common names Cutleaf Fleabane and Cutleaf Daisy. Fleabanes and Asters are often confused. Fleabanes generally have narrower, more numerous ray florets than Asters. In addition, if you check the involucral bract – the small green cup under the flower – and see that all of the bracts are the same length, then you have a Fleabane. If some of the bracts are obviously shorter, you have an Aster.

Ox-Eye Daisy

Leucanthemum vulgare (also *Chrysanthemum leucanthemum*)

COMPOSITE FAMILY

An invasive Eurasian perennial from a well developed rhizome, this plant frequents low to middle elevations in moist to moderately dry sites, like roadsides, clearings, pastures, and disturbed areas. The flowers are solitary composite heads at the end of branches, with white ray flowers and yellow disk flowers. The basal leaves are broadly lance-shaped or narrowly spoon-shaped. The stem leaves are oblong and smaller.

Daisy is from the Anglo-Saxon *day's eye*, a reference to the fact that the English daisy closes at night and opens at sun-up. One of the most common and recognizable wildflowers in North America, the Ox-Eye Daisy is very prolific, and will overgrow large areas if not kept in check. A similar flower, Scentless Chamomile (*Matricaria perforata*) occurs in similar habitat and is often confused with Ox-Eye Daisy. To confirm the identity, closely inspect the leaves on the plant in issue. Scentless Chamomile has much thinner leaflets, and they are much more dissected than are those of Ox-Eye Daisy. Another similar flower in the area is Mayweed (*Anthemis cotula*). Unlike Ox-Eye Daisy and Scentless Chamomile, Mayweed has an objectionable odour.

Palmate Coltsfoot
Petasites frigidus

COMPOSITE FAMILY

This perennial grows from a thick, creeping rhizome, putting up a white-hairy flowering stem that is up to 50 cm tall in wet to moist forests and wetlands, and along streams, rivers, and lakeshores at low to subalpine elevations. The stem appears before the leaves. The basal leaves are kidney-shaped to round, long-stalked, hairy, and palmately lobed into five to seven sharply toothed segments. The stem leaves are very much reduced to reddish bracts. The inflorescence occurs as a flat-topped cluster of composite heads at the top of the stem. The flower heads have white to pinkish ray and disk florets, or may appear with disk florets only. The flower heads have woolly-hairy bases.

The genus name, *Petasites*, is derived from the Greek *petasos*, which means "broad-brimmed hat," a reference to the large leaves. The species name, *frigidus*, is Latin meaning "stiff," most probably a reference to the stiff hairs on the plant. The flowering stem of the plant arises from a different point on the rhizome than do the leaves, so their association may not be obvious. Native peoples used the plants as food, consuming the young leaves as pot herbs. They also burned he leaves of the plant, and used the ashes as a salt substitute. Members of the genus have long been used in herbal medicine to treat coughs, asthma, and colic. The leaves were also used in poultices for wounds and inflammations. The leaves yield a yellowish-green dye.

Pathfinder Plant (Trail Plant)
Adenocaulon bicolor

COMPOSITE FAMILY

This plant grows in shady and open woods at low to moderate elevations. The basal leaves are alternate, up to 30 cm long and 15 cm wide, triangular to heart-shaped, narrowly scalloped, and appear on slender stems that reach 1 m long. The leaves are green above and white woolly below. The flowering stem is solitary with many branches, and rises above the leaves. The inconspicuous white flowers occur in small heads in a panicle at the ends of the flowering stems. The flowers have disk florets only, no ray florets. The fruits are hooked achenes that cling to clothing or fur of passersby.

The genus name, *Adenocaulon*, is derived from the Greek *adenas*, which means "gland," and *kaulos*, which means "stem," a reference to the glandular hairs on the stems of the plant. The species name refers to the distinctive two colours of the opposite leaf surfaces. The common names originate from this distinctive feature. When a hiker or other stroller moves through the plants, the leaves invert, showing the silvery white undersides. If the hiker looks back on the route taken, the path is obvious by the line of white leaves showing the trail.

Pearly Everlasting
Anaphalis margaritacea

COMPOSITE FAMILY

This plant grows in gravelly open woods and subalpine meadows in the mountains. There are numerous stem leaves, alternately attached directly to the stem. The leaves are lance-shaped and light green, with very soft fuzzy hairs. The white flowers occur in a dense, rounded terminal cluster. The male and female flowers occur on separate plants. The flowers have only disk flowers, no ray flowers, and often have a brown spot at the base.

The genus name, *Anaphalis*, is thought to be an invention of Carolus Linnaeus, relating this genus to a somewhat related genus, *Gnaphalium*, which name was, in turn, derived from the Greek *knaphalon*, which means a "tuft of wool." It could be said that the flowers of this species resemble tufts of wool. The common name, Pearly Everlasting, comes from the fact that the dried flowers resemble pearls and often last for a long time. The species name, *margaritacea*, means "of pearls," and is undoubtedly a reference to the shape of the flowers. The plant resembles Pussytoes (*Antennaria* spp.) but has more leaves, and the leaves are not reduced in size from the base to the top of the plant as they are in most Pussytoes.

Silver-Back (Silverback Luina)
Luina hypoleuca

COMPOSITE FAMILY

Dave Ingram image

This branching perennial grows on open rocky slopes and in cliff crevices from middle to subalpine elevations. The leaves are alternate, numerous, sessile, elliptic, smooth on the margins, and 3 cm long. They are dark green above and silver-white-hairy below, giving the plant its common name. The flower stems are up to 35 cm tall, and the white to pale yellow flower heads appear in numbers together in a flat cluster atop the stems. There are only disk flowers, no ray flowers.

The genus name, *Luina*, is an anagram of *Inula*, another genus in the Composite Family whose members are native to Europe, Asia, and Africa. The species name, *hypoleuca*, means "pale or whitish beneath," a reference to the leaves of this plant being different colours on their top and bottom surfaces. When a breeze buffets the plant, the leaves appear white as they shake in the wind.

White-Flowered Hawkweed
Hieracium albiflorum

COMPOSITE FAMILY

This plant is common to moist to dry open woods, meadows, and clearings at low to middle elevations. The white flower heads appear in an open inflorescence on ascending stalks. The flowers are composed entirely of ray florets, with no disk florets. The leaves are broadly lance-shaped, and often have wavy-toothed edges with bristly hairs on the upper surfaces.

The origin of the genus name, *Hieracium,* is discussed in the note on Orange Hawkweed (*H. aurantiacum*), shown on page 10. The species name, *albiflorum*, means "white flowered." The leaves, stems, and roots of all members of the genus produce a milky latex when broken.

Bunchberry (Dwarf Dogwood)
Cornus canadensis

DOGWOOD FAMILY

This is a plant of moist coniferous woods, often found on rotting logs and stumps. The flowers are clusters of inconspicuous greenish-white flowers set among four white, petal-like, showy bracts. The leaves are in a terminal whorl of four to seven, all prominently veined. The leaves are dark green above and lighter underneath. The fruits are bright red berries.

The genus name, *Cornus*, is Latin for "horn" or "antler," possibly a reference to the hard wood of some members of this genus. Another school of thought is that the inflorescence of the plant bears a resemblance to the cornice piece, a knob on cylinders used for rolling up manuscripts. *Canadensis* is a reference to Canada, this plant being widely distributed across the country in the boreal forests. Bunchberry's common name is probably derived from the fact that the fruits are all bunched together in a terminal cluster. A Nootka legend has it that the Bunchberry arose from the blood of a woman marooned in a cedar tree by her jealous husband. The plant is reported to have an explosive pollination mechanism wherein the petals of the mature but unopened flower buds suddenly reflex and the anthers spring out, casting pollen loads into the air. When an insect brushes against the tiny bristle at the end of one petal, it triggers this explosion.

Pacific Dogwood (Western Flowering Dogwood)
Cornus nuttallii

DOGWOOD FAMILY

This is an irregularly branched deciduous tree that reaches heights of up to 20 m. The bark is smooth and blackish-brown, becoming ridged with age. The leaves are opposite, oval, stalked, and pointed at the ends, with distinctive paired veins that curve parallel to the leaf margins. The leaves are dark green above, and greyish-brown below, turning to gorgeous reds in the autumn. The tree flowers in the spring with tremendous numbers of large cream-coloured blossoms. The flowers individually are small, greenish-white, numerous and inconspicuous, occurring in spherical clusters that are surrounded by four to seven very conspicuous white (sometimes pink-fringed), petal-like, showy bracts. Some individual plants might flower a second time in the fall. The fruits are clusters of brilliantly scarlet drupes.

The origin of the genus name, *Cornus*, is discussed in the note on Bunchberry (*C. canadensis*), shown on page 91. The species name, *nuttallii*, honours Thomas Nuttall, a 19th-century English naturalist. It is said that the plant was originally "discovered" by David Douglas, a Scottish explorer and botanist, but Douglas identified it as *C. florida*, an eastern, related species. Nuttall re-examined the plant later and found it to be a different species, and the species was then named in his honour by John James Audubon. Native peoples made extensive use of the plant, fashioning a variety of tools – bows, arrows, baskets, tool handles, combs, needles, hooks, and harpoons – from its close-grained, hard wood. The plant also produced a rich, dark-brown dye, and was used in various medicinal concoctions. Pacific Dogwood is the floral emblem of the province of British Columbia.

Red-Osier Dogwood
Cornus stolonifera

DOGWOOD FAMILY

This willow-like shrub that grows up to 3 m high, often forming impenetrable thickets along streams and in moist forests. The reddish bark is quite distinctive, and it becomes even redder with the advent of frosts. The leaves are heavily veined, dark green above and pale underneath. The flowers are small, greenish-white, and occur in a flat-topped cluster at the terminal ends of stems. The fruits are small white berries, appearing in clumps.

The origin of the genus name, *Cornus*, is discussed in the note on Bunchberry (*C. canadensis*), shown on page 91. The common name, Osier, appears to be from the Old French *osiere*, meaning "that which grows in an osier-bed (streambed)." Native peoples used the branches of the plant to fashion fish traps, poles, and salmon stretchers. This plant is extremely important winter browse for moose.

Enchanter's Nightshade
Circaea alpina

EVENING PRIMROSE FAMILY

This plant grows from a slender rhizome in deep shady woods at moderate elevations. The flowering stems are erect to spreading, simple, branched, hairy, and thin, growing up to 50 cm tall. The leaves are opposite, heart- to egg-shaped, 6 cm long, slightly toothed, hairy on the lower surface, and have pointed tips. The inflorescence is terminal clusters of 8 to 12 flowers. The small individual flowers are white to pale pink, have two deeply notched petals, two sepals that are bent downward, and two-lobed stigmas. The fruits are teardrop-shaped capsules that are densely covered with soft, hooked hairs that cling to clothing or fur of passers-by.

In the words of the incomparable naturalist Lewis J. Clark: "The only impressive feature of this physically insignificant plant is its name." Indeed, it is quite a name. The genus name, *Circaea*, is a reference to Circe, the enchantress of Greek mythology who used a potion to turn Odysseus' men into animals. Some early botanists speculated that this plant was the source of the potion, but that case was never proven. The reference to *alpina* in the specific name is very peculiar, given that the plant has nothing whatsoever to do with the alpine. Further, the common name Nightshade is puzzling, given that the plant bears no resemblance to the Nightshades, a member of which genus is Bittersweet (*Solanum dulcamara*), shown on page 210.

Sickletop Lousewort (Parrot's Beak)
Pedicularis racemosa

FIGWORT FAMILY

This lovely plant favours upper montane and subalpine environments. The white flower has a very distinctive shape that deserves close examination to appreciate its intricacy. The flowers appear along a purplish-coloured stem that grows up to 35 cm tall. The leaves are simple, lance-shaped to linear, and have distinctive fine, sharp teeth on the margins.

The origin of the genus name, *Pedicularis*, is explained in the narrative on Bracted Lousewort (*P. bracteosa*), shown on page 248. The common name, Sickletop Lousewort, is a reference to the shape of the flowers. Another common name, Parrot's Beak, arises from the long, slender downward-turned beak on the upper lip of the petals. The plant is said to have been first collected for science by 19th-century Scottish explorer and botanist David Douglas in 1830.

Devil's Club
Oplopanax horridus

GINSENG FAMILY

If there were a contest for the meanest plant in the woods, this one would almost certainly qualify. Devil's Club is aptly named. It has club-shaped woody stems that grow to over 2 m tall, and the stems are covered in stiff, sharp spines. The leaves are large, shaped like very large maple leaves, with sharp spines on their veins and leaf stalks, and sharp teeth on their margins. The flowers are small, white, and globe-shaped, and are arranged along a central flower stalk up to 25 cm long. The fruits are a mass of shiny red berries.

The genus name, *Oplopanax*, is derived from the Greek *hoplon*, meaning "weapon." The species name, *horridus*, comes from the same root as "horrible." The spines of the plant easily break off in skin, and the punctures occasioned will quickly become sore and inflamed. In spite of all this, the plant is quite handsome and regal. It also has a number of medicinal properties, and has been used by Native peoples and herbalists to treat such diverse ailments as arthritis, diabetes, cataracts, and indigestion. It is recommended that this plant be given a good inspection, but do not get too close.

Wild Sarsaparilla
Aralia nudicaulis

GINSENG FAMILY

This plant prefers the dark woods of the moist montane forests. It is common east of the coastal mountains, but does also occur on Vancouver Island. The leaves are up to 50 cm long, arising singly from an underground stem. Each leaf has a long, bare stalk that terminates in three to five leaflets each. The leaflets are up to 15 cm long, and are sharply toothed and pointed at the ends. The flowers arise from a short stem near ground level, well below the spreading leaflets. The flowers are tiny, whitish-green, and arranged in three round umbels.

The genus name, *Aralia*, is the Latinized form of the French *aralie*, the Quebec *habitant* name for the plant. The species name, *nudicaulis*, means "bare stem," a reference to the leafless flower stalk. The plant was used as stimulant in sweat lodges by some Native peoples, and was also used in a variety of other medicinal ways.

Fringed Grass-of-Parnassus
Parnassia fimbriata

GRASS-OF-PARNASSUS FAMILY

These plants abound in riverine habitat, pond edges, and boggy places from montane to the subalpine zone. The white flowers are very delicate-looking. The flowers appear as singles on a slender stem, with five white petals and greenish or yellowish veins. The lower edges of the petals are fringed with hairs. Alternating fertile and sterile stamens are characteristic of this genus. The leaves are mostly basal and broadly kidney-shaped. A single leaf clasps the flowering stem about halfway up.

The name of this plant seems to present some confusion. One school of thought is that the genus name, *Parnassia*, is from Mount Parnassus in Greece, said to be a favourite retreat of the god Apollo. Another school of thought holds that the name comes from a description of the plant written in the 1st century by Dioscorides, a military physician for the Roman emperor Nero. When the description was translated, "grass" was included in the translation, and it stuck. There is no doubt that this plant is not even remotely grass-like. A similar species, Northern Grass-of-Parnassus (*P. palustris*) occurs in the similar habitat, but it does not have the fringed margins of Fringed Grass-of-Parnassus.

Greenish-Flowered Wintergreen (Green Wintergreen)
Pyrola chlorantha (also *P. virens*)

HEATH FAMILY

This is an erect perennial that inhabits moist to dry coniferous and mixed forests, and riverine environments, from the montane to the subalpine zones. The flowers have five greenish-white, waxy petals, and a long style attached to a prominent ovary. The flowers have a bell shape and are distributed on short stalks up the main stem. The leaves are basal, in a rosette. The leaves have a leathery appearance and are shiny, rounded, and dark green.

The genus name, *Pyrola*, is derived from Latin *pyrus*, which means "a pear," probably a reference to the leaves being pear-shaped. Wintergreen leaves contain acids that are effective in treating skin irritations. Mashed leaves of *Pyrola* species have traditionally been used by herbalists in skin salves, and poultices for snake and insect bites. They are called wintergreen, not because of the taste, but because the leaves remain green during the winter. Like orchids, these plants require a specific fungus in the soil to grow successfully, and transplantation should not be attempted. Another species of *Pyrola*, Pink Wintergreen, (*P. asarifolia*), shown on page 36, is similar in shape and occurs in similar habitat, but has pink flowers.

Hairy Manzanita
Arctostaphylos columbiana

HEATH FAMILY

This is an erect to spreading evergreen shrub with smooth reddish bark that grows up to 3 m tall in sunny, open places and rocky outcrops along the coast. The leaves are ovate to elliptic, 2–5 cm long and half as wide, have pointed tips, and appear grey-green owing to a mat of grey hairs on both sides of the leaves. The flowers are white to pink, urn-shaped, up to 6 mm long, and occur in clusters at the ends of the branches. The fruits are coffee-coloured berries.

The origin of the genus name, *Arctostaphylos*, is explained in the note on Bearberry (*A. uva-ursi*), shown on page 25. The species name, *columbiana*, is a reference to western North America. The common name, Manzanita, is derived from Spanish, and means "little apples," a reference to the fruits.

Indian Pipe (Ghost Plant)
Monotropa uniflora

HEATH FAMILY

This unique and unusual plant grows either solitary or in clumps from a dense root system, and occurs in moist, shaded woods in rich soil. It is fairly rare and is said to appear almost overnight, like a mushroom. Instead of leaves, it has colourless scales. The flowers are white to cream-coloured, nodding on stems up to 20 cm tall and shaped like a smoking pipe stuck into the ground by its stem. The flowers darken to black with age, and turn upward at the top of the stem. Stems from the previous year's growth may persist.

The genus name, *Monotropa*, is derived from the Greek *monos*, meaning "single," and *tropos*, meaning "direction," a reference to the flowers being turned to one side. This plant contains no chlorophyll and is saprophytic, meaning it obtains its nutrients from dead and decaying plant or animal matter. Native peoples used the plant for a number of medicinal purposes. Other common names applied to the plant are Ghost Flower, Corpse Plant, and Ice Plant. Another member of the genus, Pine-Sap (*M. hypopithys*) exists in similar habitat, but it is rarer yet. It has numerous urn-shaped, light brown to cream-coloured flowers on its stem.

Labrador Tea
Ledum groenlandicum

HEATH FAMILY

This evergreen, much-branched shrub is widespread in low to subalpine elevations in peaty wetlands and moist coniferous forests. The flowers are white and numerous, with five to ten protruding stamens in umbrella-like clusters at the ends of branches. The leaves are alternate and narrow, with edges rolled under. They are deep green and leathery on top, with dense rusty hairs underneath.

The genus name, *Ledum*, is derived from the Greek *ledon*, which means "mastic," the Greek name for an Old World plant whose foliage resembles that of this species. The leaves, used fresh or dried, can be brewed into an aromatic tea, but should be used in moderation to avoid drowsiness. Excessive doses are reported to act as a strong diuretic. The aromatic leaves were used in barns to drive away mice, and in houses to keep away fleas.

Menzies' Pipsissewa (Little Prince's Pine)
Chimaphila menziesii

HEATH FAMILY

This dwarf evergreen shrub grows to 15 cm tall in coniferous woods at low to middle elevations. The dark greenish-blue, glossy leaves are alternate, lance-shaped to oval, and toothed on the margins. The one to three flowers are creamy white, waxy, saucer-shaped and nodding on an erect stem above the leaves. The fruits of the plant are dry, round, brown capsules that often overwinter on the stem, as shown in the photo above.

This plant is a smaller version of Pipsissewa or Prince's Pine (*C. umbellata*), shown on page 37. The genus name, *Chimaphila*, and the common name Pipsissewa are explained in the note on that plant. The distinctive features on this plant are its more diminutive size, white flowers, and leaves that are alternate, not whorled. The specific name of this plant honours Dr. Archibald Menzies, an 18th-century Scottish physician and botanist who accompanied Captain George Vancouver on some of his explorations to the Pacific Northwest.

One-Sided Wintergreen
Pyrola secunda (also *Orthilia secunda*)

HEATH FAMILY

This small forest dweller grows to 5–15 cm tall at low to subalpine elevations in dry to moist coniferous or mixed woods and clearings. The white to yellowish-green flowers lie on one side of the arching stalk, arranged in a raceme of six to ten flowers, sometimes more. The flowers resemble small street lights strung along a curving pole. The straight style sticks out beyond the petals, with a flat, five-lobed stigma. The leaves are basal, egg-shaped, and finely toothed at the margins.

One-Sided Wintergreen is included in the *Pyrola* genus by some taxonomists but is put into the *Orthilia* genus by others. The origin of the genus name, *Pyrola*, is explained in the note on Greenish-Flowered Wintergreen (*P. chlorantha*), shown on page 99. *Orthilia* is derived from the Greek *orthos*, meaning "straight," most probably a reference to the straight style. The species name, *secunda*, is Latin meaning "next" or "following," a reference to the flowers which follow each other on the same side of the stem. The plant also goes by the aptly descriptive, locally common name Sidebells Winter-green. Once seen, this delightful little flower is unmistakable in the woods.

Painted Pyrola (White-Veined Wintergreen)
Pyrola picta

HEATH FAMILY

This erect perennial inhabits moist coniferous and mixed forests. The flowers are similar to Greenish-Flowered Wintergreen (*P. chlorantha*), shown on page 99 – bell shaped, waxy and distributed along the main stalk – but the leaf of this plant is the distinguishing feature. The leaves of Painted Pyrola are thick, glossy, and green, with extraordinarily beautiful white mottling along the veins of the upper surface. This mottling gives the plant its other common name, White-Veined Wintergreen. The pale areas on the leaf's surface are caused by a lack of chlorophyll, which indicates the partially parasitic nature of the plant.

The origin of the genus name, *Pyrola*, is discussed in the note on Greenish-Flowered Wintergreen, shown on page 99. The species name, *picta*, means "painted" or "brightly coloured," no doubt a reference to the leaves. The plant also goes by the locally common name Nootka Wintergreen, a reference to Nootka Sound or Nootka Island, British Columbia, where the plant apparently was first discovered. Wintergreen leaves contain acids which are effective in treating skin irritations. Like orchids, these plants require a specific fungus in the soil to grow successfully and transplantation should not be attempted. Another species of *Pyrola*, Pink Wintergreen, (*P. asarifolia*), shown on page 36, is similar in shape and occurs in similar habitat, but has pink flowers.

Single Delight
Moneses uniflora (also *Pyrola uniflora*)

HEATH FAMILY

This delightful little forest dweller is also known as One-Flowered Winter-green, and it inhabits damp forests, usually on rotting wood. The plant is quite tiny, standing only 15 cm tall, and the single white flower, open and nodding at the top of the stem, is less than 5 cm in diameter. The flower looks like a small white umbrella, offering shade. The leaves are basal, oval, and evergreen, attached to the base of the stem. The style is prominent and tipped with a five-lobed stigma that almost looks like a mechanical part of some kind.

The genus name, *Moneses*, is derived from the Greek *monos*, meaning "solitary," and *hesia*, meaning "delight," a reference to the delightful single flower. Other common names include Wood Nymph and Shy Maiden. In Greek mythology, nymphs were nature goddesses, beautiful maidens living in rivers, woods, and mountains, and once you see this diminutive flower, the common names seem completely appropriate.

Western Tea-Berry
Gaultheria ovatifolia

HEATH FAMILY

Virginia Skilton images

This evergreen shrub is sprawling and ground-hugging, only 5 cm tall, and occurs in a variety of habitat from open ponderosa pine forests, to cold bogs, to subalpine slopes. The stems on the plant are very thin, brownish, and hairy. The leaves are glossy, alternate, egg- to heart-shaped with saw-toothed margins, and grow up to 4 cm long. The white/cream or pink flowers are small, bell- or urn-shaped, nodding, and hairy. They occur singly in the axils of the leaves.

The genus name, *Gaultheria*, honours Dr. Jean-François Gaultier, an 18th-century French-Canadian physician and naturalist. The species name, *ovatifolia*, is a reference to the shape of the leaves of the plant. The plant goes by several locally common names, including Oregon Spicy Wintergreen, Oregon Wintergreen, Mountain Checkerberry, and Western Wintergreen. Creeping Snowberry (*G. hispidula*) is a related plant that grows in the region. It is a creeping, matted evergreen that has pinkish, bell-shaped flowers, but its fruits are white, juicy, edible berries.

White Heather (White Mountain Heather)
Cassiope mertensiana

HEATH FAMILY

Doug Skilton image

This matting plant occurs in the subalpine and alpine zones. The flowers are white, bell-shaped and nodding at the end of the stems. The leaves are opposite, evergreen, and pressed so closely to the stems that the stems are all but hidden. The foliage forms low mats on the ground.

The genus name, *Cassiope*, is from Greek mythology. Cassiopeia was the wife of Cepheus, the King of the Ethiopians. She was vain and boastful, claiming that her beauty exceeded that of the sea nymphs. This claim offended and angered the sea nymphs, and they prevailed upon Poseidon, the god of the sea, to send a sea monster to punish Cassiopeia by ravaging the land. In order to save the kingdom, the Ethiopians offered Cassiopeia's daughter, Andromeda, as a sacrifice, chaining her to a rock. Perseus, the Greek hero who slew the Gorgon Medusa, intervened at the last minute to free Andromeda and slay the monster. In astronomy, the constellation Perseus stands between Cassiopeia and Andromeda, still defending her today. While interesting, what all that has to do with this flower is a mystery. The species name, *mertensiana*, honours F.C. Mertens, an early German botanist. In fact, White Mountain Heather is not a heather at all, but a heath.

White Rhododendron
Rhododendron albiflorum

HEATH FAMILY

This is an erect and spreading deciduous shrub that grows up to 2 m tall and inhabits cool, damp woods, often establishing dense communities under the conifer canopy. The leaves are oblong to lance-shaped, and are covered with fine rusty-coloured hairs. The leaves turn to beautiful shades of crimson and orange in the fall. The flowers are large (up to 3 cm across), white, and cup-shaped, and are borne singly or in small clusters around the stem of the previous year's growth. The petals are joined to each other for about half of their length, and there are 10 stamens visible inside the flower. The flowers are deciduous, and fall off of the plant as a whole, often littering the forest floor with what appear to be intact flowers.

The genus name, *Rhododendron*, is derived from the Greek *rhodon*, meaning "rose," and *dendron*, meaning "tree." The species name, *albiflorum*, is Latin meaning "white-flowered." This plant is often referred to as Mountain Misery because it grows in dense communities, with branches trailing downhill, making it difficult for hikers to move through it. The plant also has the locally common name Cascade Azalea. All parts of the plant contain poisonous alkaloids that are toxic to humans and livestock.

Low-Bush Cranberry (Mooseberry)
Viburnum edule

HONEYSUCKLE FAMILY

This plant is a sprawling deciduous shrub that grows up to 2 m tall, from low to subalpine elevations in moist to wet forests, along streams, and in boggy areas. The leaves are opposite, sharply toothed, and maple-leaf shaped with three lobes. The tiny, white, five-parted flowers appear in flat-topped showy clusters between leaves along the stem. The fruits are clusters of red or orange berries that contain a large, flattened stone. The fruits remain on the plant after the leaves fall, and the over-ripe berries and decaying leaves often produce a musty odour in the woods near the plants.

The genus name, *Viburnum*, is the classical Latin for an Old World member of the genus. The species name, *edule*, means "edible," and refers to the fruits of the plant. The fruits are favoured by birds. The fruits were used extensively by Native peoples as food, and other parts of the plant were used medicinally. In the fall the leaves of this plant turn beautiful crimson and purple colours. Two other locally common names for the plant are Mooseberry and Squash-berry. Some confusion can arise because of the existence of a plant called a High-Bush Cranberry (*V. trilobum*), which occurs in similar habitat. That plant is a larger bush – almost a small tree – with similar flowers and fruits. Neither the Low-Bush or the High-Bush are truly Cranberries, which are members of the Heath Family.

Red Elderberry
Sambucus racemosa var. *arborescens*

HONEYSUCKLE FAMILY

This is a tall deciduous shrub that grows to several metres tall, occurring from low to subalpine elevations along streams, in moist thickets and clearings, and in shady forests. The opposite, branching stems of the plant are woody, stout, and filled with pith in the centre. The leaves are pinnately compound, with five to seven leaflets that are pointed, lance-shaped, and sharply toothed. The flowers are white to creamy in colour, and occur in large pyramid-shaped clusters. The flowers have a relatively strong unpleasant odour. The fruits are red berries that appear in the late summer.

The genus name, *Sambucus*, is from the Greek *sambuke*, a musical instrument made from elderwood. The fruits of this plant have long been used as food. Wine and jellies can be produced from the berries. Bears and birds seem quite partial to the fruits. The branches of the plant have been hollowed out to make whistles, drinking straws, pipe stems, and blowguns, but that practice is discouraged because the branches of the plant contain glycosides and are poisonous. The common name Elder is said to be derived from the Anglo-Saxon *aeld*, which means "to kindle," a reference to the hollow stems of the plant being used to blow on tinder to start a fire. Another Elderberry that occurs in the same range – Blue Elderberry (*S. cerulea*) – has waxy, blue fruits. Black Elderberry (*S. racemosa* var. *melanocarpa*), is fairly common in the Rocky Mountains. It has black fruits.

Red Twinberry (Utah Honeysuckle)
Lonicera utahensis

HONEYSUCKLE FAMILY

This erect deciduous shrub grows up to 2 m tall at low to subalpine elevations in moist to wet forest openings and clearings in the southern portion of the region. The leaves are opposite, elliptical to oblong, with smooth edges and blunt tips. The creamy-white flowers are trumpet-shaped and appear in pairs on a single stalk from the leaf axils. The fruits are red berries that are joined at the base.

The origin of the genus name, *Lonicera*, is discussed in the note on Black Twinberry (*L. involucrata*), shown on page 256. The specific name, *utahensis*, refers to the State of Utah, where the first specimen of the plant was collected for scientific description. Some Native peoples ate the berries, which were said to be a good emergency source of water because they are so juicy. The flowers are frequented by hummingbirds, which are said to use the flower extensively for food. The plant is also known as Utah Honeysuckle.

Mock Orange
Philadelphus lewisii

HYDRANGEA FAMILY

Virginia Skilton image

This stiff and densely branched, erect deciduous shrub grows up to 3 m tall in thickets, on rocky hillsides, in crevices and along streams from valley to subalpine elevations. The leaves occur in opposite pairs on the stems, and the bark of the shrub is reddish-brown to grey. The plant flowers in the late spring, producing lots of white flowers, which have four oblong white petals, four styles and many stamens. The flower emits a sweet, orange-blossom aroma. The fruits are hard capsules that overwinter on the shrub.

There is some disagreement among the authorities as to how this plant got its scientific name. One school of thought has it that the genus name, *Philadelphus*, has its origins in the Greek *philos*, which means "friend," and *adelphos*, meaning "brother," thus, approximately, "brotherly love," as in the motto of the city of Philadelphia, Pennsylvania. The other school of thought attributes the genus name to a commemoration of the Pharaoh Ptolemy II Philadelphus. The species name honours Meriwether Lewis, who first collected a specimen of the plant in 1806 along the Clearwater River in present-day Idaho. Mock Orange is the floral emblem of the State of Idaho. The plant often goes by the locally common name of Syringa, which is puzzling because that name is the genus name for lilacs, which are a totally unrelated plant.

Bronzebells
Stenanthium occidentale

LILY FAMILY

This lily of moist woods, stream banks, meadows, and slopes has grass-like leaves that emerge from an onion-like bulb. The bell-shaped flowers are greenish-white, flecked with purple, and have six sharply pointed tips that twist backward, exposing the interior of the blossom. Ten or more graceful and fragrant flowers are hung along the length of the stem, drooping down.

The genus name, *Stenanthium*, is derived from the Greek *stenos*, meaning "narrow," and *anthos*, meaning "flower." The appropriateness of this name will be testified to by any photographer who has tried to photograph this species in even a slight breeze. The species name, *occidentale*, means "western." Without question, this flower is extraordinarily attractive in its detail. Apparently some Native peoples believed the plant to be poisonous. Some authorities say it is; others say it is not. The plant also goes by the locally common names Mountain Bells and Western Mountainbells.

Clasping-Leaved Twisted-Stalk
Streptopus amplexifolius

LILY FAMILY

This plant grows in moist, shaded forests and has a widely branching zigzag stem with numerous sharp-pointed, parallel-veined leaves that encircle the stem at each angular bend. The plant varies in height from 30–100 cm. The glossy leaves often conceal the small, pale white or greenish flowers that dangle on curving, thread-like stalks from the axil of each of the upper leaves. In fact, one can walk by the plant without noticing the flowers hiding under the leaves. The flowers have strongly reflexed petals and sepals, and appear to be hanging on the plant like small spiders dangling on fine webs. The fruits of the plant are very handsome, orangish-red, oval berries.

The genus name, *Streptopus*, is derived from the Greek *streptos*, meaning "twisted," and *pous*, meaning "foot," referring to the twisted flower stalks. The species name, *amplexifolius*, is derived from the Latin *amplexor*, meaning "to surround," and *folius*, meaning "a leaf." Two other members of the genus occur in the region. Rosy Twisted Stalk (*S. roseus*) is a smaller plant with a stem that is unbranched and not conspicuously bent, and has rose-coloured bell-shaped flowers with white tips. Small Twisted Stalk (*S. streptopoides*) is smaller yet, has unbranched stems, and rose to purplish flowers that are saucer-shaped with the petal tips curled back.

Death Camas (Meadow Death Camas)
Zigadenus venenosus

LILY FAMILY

This plant of moist grasslands, grassy slopes, and open woods grows from an onion-like bulb that has no oniony smell. The leaves are mainly basal and resemble grass, with prominent midveins.

The greenish-white, foul-smelling flowers appear in tight clusters atop an erect stem, each flower having three virtually identical petals and sepals. There are yellowish-green, V-shaped glands (nectaries) near the base of the petals and sepals.

The genus name, *Zigadenus*, is derived from the Greek *zygos*, meaning "yoke," and *adenas*, meaning "gland," a reference to the shape of the nectary at the base of each petal and sepal. The species name, *venenosus*, is Latin for "very poisonous." Death Camas contains poisonous alkaloids, and is probably even more toxic than its close relative, White Camas (*Z. elegans*), which occurs in areas east of the coastal mountains. These plants have been responsible for killing many people and animals. When the flowers are absent, Death Camas and White Camas are difficult to distinguish from Early Camas (*Camassia quamas*), shown on page 203, the bulb of which was commonly used as food by Native peoples and early settlers. Failure to make this distinction was deadly.

Fairybells
Prosartes hookeri (formerly *Disporum hookeri*)

LILY FAMILY

A plant of moist shaded woods, stream banks, and riverine environments, this delightful flower blooms in early summer. The flowers have six tepals, and are bell-shaped, creamy white, and occur in drooping pairs at the end of branches. The leaves of the plant are generally lance-shaped with parallel veins and pointed ends. The fruits are reddish-orange egg-shaped berries, occurring in pairs.

While once in the genus *Disporum*, North American members of the genus were recently moved to the genus *Prosartes*, leaving only Eastern Asian species in the former genus. The genus name, *Prosartes*, is derived from the Greek *prosartes*, which means "attached," a reference to the manner in which the fruits are attached. The species name, *hookeri*, honours Joseph Dalton Hooker, who is considered by many to be the most important botanist of the 19th century. The plant is also known by the locally common names Hooker's Fairybells and Oregon Drops Of Gold. The fruits of Fairybells are edible, but said to be bland. They are a favoured food of many rodents and birds. Large-Flowered Fairybells (*P. smithii*) is a relatively rarer related species that occurs in the similar habitat in the area. Its flowers are larger, cream-coloured, and its petals and sepals form a cylinder, with only the tips spread outward.

False Lily-of-the-Valley (Western Lily-of-the-Valley)
Maianthemum dilatatum

LILY FAMILY

This lily rises from a creeping, running rhizome along creeks and in areas of extensive rainfall in the western coastal area and ranges, often forming very large colonies. It typically has two large, long-stalked, heart-shaped leaves per stem, each 5–10 cm long and about as wide. The inflorescence occurs as a cylindrical raceme of 10 to 50 fragrant white flowers on an upright stem 40 cm tall. Unlike most other lilies that have flower parts in threes, this one – and related Wild Lily-of-the-Valley (*M. canadense*) – has parts in twos, with each flower having four similar tepals. The fruits are red berries.

This species is called False because true Lily-of-the-Valley (*Convallaria majalis*) is a European species that has white, nodding, bell-shaped, six-tepalled flowers. The allied species Wild Lily-of-the-Valley grows east of the Selkirk range. Its leaves appear on shorter stalks, and they taper more abruptly than those of False Lily-of-the-Valley.

The genus name, *Maianthemum*, literally translates from Latin as Mayflower. And in fact, to further confuse things, False and Western Lily-of-the-Valley are often referred to as Mayflower, a name that is commonly associated with the totally unrelated species Trailing Arbutus (*Epigaea repens*). Lily-of-the-Valley is an object lesson in how quickly and thoroughly common names can confuse things.

False Solomon's-Seal
Maianthemum racemosum (formerly *Smilacina racemosa*)

LILY FAMILY

A lily of moist woods, rivers and stream banks, thickets, and meadows, that can grow up to half a metre tall. The flowers are small and white, arranged in a branching panicle that is upright at the end of the stem. The leaves are broadly lance-shaped, numerous and alternate, gradually tapering to a pointed tip, with prominent parallel veining, sometimes folded at the midline. The fruit is a red berry flecked with maroon.

This plant was formerly in the genus *Smilacina*, but has now been moved to the genus *Maianthemum* as a result of molecular data establishing similarity to that different genus. *Maianthemum* is Latin for "May flower." The species name, *racemosum*, indicates that the plant has a raceme arrangement for the flowers. This name is somewhat confusing in that a raceme is an unbranched cluster of flowers on a common stalk. The flower arrangement on this plant is more precisely referred to as a panicle – a branched flower cluster that blooms from the bottom up. A very similar plant lives in the same habitat – the Star-Flowered Solomon's-Seal (*M. stellatum*), shown on page 124 – but it has significantly fewer flowers, which are shaped like six-sided stars.

Fool's Onion (White Triteleia)
Triteleia hyacinthina (also *Brodiaea hyacinthina*)

LILY FAMILY

This plant grows from a scaly, globe-shaped corm that occurs in open grasslands and meadows at low elevations. The corm sends up an erect, smooth, slender, leafless, flowering stem (scape) that grows to 60 cm tall. There are one or two thin, linear, basal leaves that are almost as tall as the scape. The inflorescence is a compact umbel of 5–20 white flowers. Each individual flower is bell-shaped, white, often tinged in blue, with a vivid greenish-blue line marking the backs of the petals and sepals. Though the inflorescence resembles that of an onion, this plant is not an onion and does not give off any oniony odour, thus the common name.

The genus names *Triteleia* and *Brodiaea* appear to be synonymous. In fact, two locally common names for this plant are White Brodiaea and White Triteleia. *Triteleia* is derived from the Greek *tri*, meaning "three," and *teleios*, meaning "perfect," a reference to the floral parts being in threes. *Brodiaea* honours 19th-century Scottish botanist James Brodie. The species name, *hyacinthina*, means "light violet to purplish in colour." Howell's Triteleia (*T. howellii*) is a related plant that appears in the same habitat. It has blue flowers.

Indian Hellebore (False Hellebore)
Veratrum viride

LILY FAMILY

This is a tall, stout, often fuzzy-haired perennial with many leaves that inhabits moist forests, thickets, bogs, wet meadows and avalanche chutes. The greenish flowers are somewhat inconspicuous and occur in long, open, drooping clusters along a substantial stalk that arises from the centre of the generally basal leaves. The stamens are yellow-tipped. Perhaps the most distinctive feature of this robust plant is the leaves. They are large, dull green, with long, closed sheaths at the base. Each leaf is broadly elliptic with a pointed tip, and has a prominently veined or ribbed smooth surface above and a hairy underside. The basal leaves appear well before the flowers, and seem to whirl up from the earth, dwarfing all other plants around them.

This plant is also known as Green False Hellebore, a reference apparently to the genus name, *Veratrum*, being used in ancient times to apply to a true hellebore, which was a member of the Helleborus Family. The genus name is derived from the Latin words *verus*, meaning "true," and *atrum*, meaning "black," a reference to the black roots of the true hellebore. The species name, *viride*, means "green." This plant contains very toxic alkaloids which can cause symptoms similar to heart attacks. People have died from eating it, and, indeed, the Blackfoot are said to have used the plant to commit suicide. The plant is most dangerous early in the growing season, and is said to have caused accidental poisonings among cattle and sheep. Early American settlers boiled the roots and combed the resulting liquid through their hair to kill lice. The plant also goes by the locally common name Corn Lily.

121

Queen's Cup
Clintonia uniflora

LILY FAMILY

This beautiful perennial lily grows from slender rhizomes, with the flowers appearing on short, leafless stalks. The flowers are about 5 cm in diameter and are usually solitary, white, and cup-shaped, appearing at the top of an erect, hairy stem. The plant has two or three leaves, which are oblong or elliptical, shiny with hairy edges, and appear at the base of the flowering stem.

The genus name, *Clintonia*, honours DeWitt Clinton, a 19th-century New York State governor and botanist. As the season progresses, the flower is replaced by a single deep blue bead-like berry, giving the plant two other locally common names of Beadlily and Bluebead Lily. The bead was used by some Native peoples to make a blue dye.

Slimleaf Onion
Allium amplectens

LILY FAMILY

This onion grows in habitats that are vernally wet but dry later in the year. The leaves are narrow, clasping on the stems, and somewhat rounded in cross-section. The leaves usually wither prior to the flower blooming. The inflorescence is a cluster of 10 to 50 white to light pink flowers that occur in a cluster atop the stem. Each flower has six distinct tepals, and the tips of the tepals do not turn up at the ends as is seen in the closely related Hooker's Onion (*A. acuminatum*), shown on page 45.

The origin of the genus name, *Allium*, is explained in the note on Nodding Onion (*A. cernuum*), shown on page 46. The species name, *amplectens*, means "embracing" or "clasping," most probably a reference to the tepals, which become papery in fruit and fold over the ovaries. The stem gives off a strong odour of onion when crushed. The plant also goes by the locally common name of Paper Onion. Slimleaf Onion occurs in the same habitat and often blooms simultaneously with Fool's Onion (*Brodiaea hyacinthina*), shown on page 120, and the two may be conflated. Fool's Onion has a bluish-green midvein on its petals which Slimleaf Onion lacks, and there is no onion odour when the stem of Fool's Onion is crushed.

Star-Flowered Solomon's-Seal
Maianthemum stellatum (formerly *Smilacina stellata*)

LILY FAMILY

This is a lily of moist woods, rivers and stream banks, thickets, and meadows, from montane to subalpine elevations. The flowers are white, star-shaped, and arrayed in a loose, short-stalked cluster, often on a zig-zag stem. The leaves are broadly lance-shaped, numerous, and alternate, gradually tapering to a pointed tip, with prominent parallel veining, sometimes folded at the midline. The fruit is a cluster of green- to cream-coloured berries, with maroon to brown stripes.

This plant was formerly in the genus *Smilacina*, but has now been moved to the genus *Maianthemum* as a result of molecular data establishing similarity to that different genus. *Maianthemum* is Latin for "May flower." One theory holds that the common name is a reference to the six-pointed star in the seal of King Solomon. The species name, *stellatum*, is Greek for "star-like." There is another closely related species found in the same habitat – False Solomon's-Seal (*M. racemosum*) – shown on page 119. The flowers of False Solomon's-Seal are much more numerous, and decidedly smaller than those of Star-Flowered Solomon's-Seal. The flowers of False Solomon's-Seal were described by one observer as a "creamy foam of flowers," a rather apt description.

Sticky False Asphodel (Northern Asphodel)
Tofieldia glutinosa

LILY FAMILY

A lily of wet bogs, meadows, and stream banks, this plant has a distinctive feature in the upper portion of its flowering stem, which is glandular and sticky. The white flowers are clustered atop the stem, with dark anthers conspicuous against the white of the petals. The basal leaves are linear, lance-shaped, and grass-like, and are about half the length of the stem.

The plant resembles the European Asphodel, thus the common name. The genus name, *Tofieldia*, is to honour 18th-century British botanist Thomas Tofield. The species name, *glutinosa*, is a reference to the sticky stem below the flower. Mosquitoes are often trapped on the sticky stem of this plant, which acts as natural flypaper.

Western Trillium (Western Wake Robin)
Trillium ovatum

LILY FAMILY

This gorgeous lily blooms early and prefers boggy, rich soils in the montane and lower subalpine forests. The distinctive leaves are large (up to 15 cm long), stalkless, broadly egg-shaped with a sharp tip, and occur in a whorl of three below the flower. The solitary white flower blooms atop a short stem above the leaves. The flower has three broad white petals up to 5 cm long, alternating with three narrow green sepals. The petals change colour with age, first turning pink, and then progressing to purple.

The common and genus names are derived from the Latin *trillium*, meaning "in threes," a reference to the leaves, petals, and sepals occurring in threes. The species name, *ovatum*, refers to the shape of the leaves. The plant is an early bloomer, which gives rise to its other common name, Wake Robin, it being said that the blooms and the robins arrive about the same time in the spring. Seeds from the plant are oil rich and attract ants. Ants carry the seeds to their nests, and thus distribute the seeds for the plant. Some Native peoples referred to the plant as "Birth Root," a reference to using the plant to reduce uterine bleeding during childbirth. The plant was first described for science by Frederick Pursh from a specimen collected in 1806 by Meriwether Lewis "on the rapids of the Columbia River." Trillium is the floral emblem of the Province of Ontario.

White Fawn Lily
Erythronium oregonum

LILY FAMILY

This early-blooming lily favours moist fields and open woods at lower elevations. The plant has two large (10–20 cm) dark green, opposite, elliptic, basal leaves that are very attractively mottled with brown or white. The large, white flower appears at the top of a leafless, smooth stem, usually as a solitary, but an individual plant may have as many as three flowers. The flowers are nodding, with six reflexed tepals that often display yellowish green, to rose-coloured, to orange/purple markings on the inner surface.

The origin of the genus name, *Erythronium,* is explained in the note on Pink Fawn Lily (*E. revolutum*), shown on page 47. Plants in this genus have a number of locally common names – Trout Lily, Dog's Tooth Violet, and Adder's Tongue – being among them. Trout Lily is said to arise because the mottled leaves resemble the markings on a trout. Dog's Tooth Violet is said to arise because the bulb (corm) is white and resembles a dog's tooth (though the plants are certainly not Violets). Adder's Tongue is said to refer to the similarity between a snake's tongue and the sharply pointed emergent leaves of the plants. Another member of the genus, Glacier Lily (*E. grandiflorum*), shown on page 257, occurs at higher elevations.

Northern Bedstraw
Galium boreale

MADDER FAMILY

This plant is common on roadsides and in woodlands in the montane to subalpine zones in the region. The flowers are tiny, fragrant, and white, occurring in dense clusters at the top of the stems. The individual flowers are cruciform (cross-shaped), with each having four spreading petals that are joined at the base. There are no sepals. The smooth stems are square in cross-section, and bear whorls of four narrow, lance-shaped leaves, each with three veins.

The genus name, *Galium*, is derived from the Greek *gala*, which means "milk," a reference to the fact that country folk used to use the juice of another similar plant to curdle milk. The species name, *boreale*, means "northern," a reference to the circumpolar distribution of the plant. The common name is a reference to a practice of Native peoples using the dried, sweet-smelling plants to stuff mattresses. The roots of the plants were a source of red and yellow dyes.

Yerba Buena
Clinopodium douglasii (formerly *Satureja douglasii*)

MINT FAMILY

This mat-forming plant is a trailing, evergreen mint, with creeping stems that might reach 1 m in length. It grows in openings in coniferous forests and mixed woods at low elevations. The stems are square in cross-section, typical of mints. The leaves occur in opposite pairs up to 3 cm long, and are oval, with blunt teeth. The small white to blue-lavender flowers occur in the leaf axils. The flowers are two-lipped, with the upper lip erect and notched, the lower one three-lobed and spreading.

The common name was given to the plant by 18th-century Spanish priests who settled in what was to become the State of California. In Spanish, Yerba Buena means "good herb," a reference to the supposed medicinal properties of the plant. San Francisco was originally called Yerba Buena by its settlers, owing to the abundance of this plant in the vicinity. The city was renamed San Francisco by the Americans when the city was captured during the Mexican-American War in 1846. An island in San Francisco Bay still goes by the original name. Native peoples used the aromatic leaves of the plant to brew a medicinal tea. The plant also goes by the locally common name Oregon Tea.

Morning Glory
Calystegia sepium (also *Convolvulus sepium*)

MORNING GLORY FAMILY

Morning Glory is a twining, climbing, or trailing vine that grows from slender, spreading rhizomes. The flowers are 3–6 cm across, white to pinkish in colour and trumpet- or funnel-shaped. The leaves are alternate and arrowhead-shaped, and the flowers appear solitary in the leaf axils. The flowers usually close when it is dark, overcast or raining.

The genus name, *Calystegia*, is derived from the Greek *kalyx*, meaning "cup" and *stegos*, meaning "cover," a reference to the bracts that cover the sepals on the flower. This plant is also commonly called Hedge Bindweed, Lady's Nightcap, and Bell-Bind. A closely related plant, Field Bindweed (*C. arvensis*), is a noxious weed that creeps over crops and covers everything within its reach. Unlike many climbing plants, the Bindweeds cannot support their stems and tendrils, so they wind their stems tightly around available supports. Under favourable conditions, a Bindweed stem will complete an encirclement of a support in less than two hours time. Another related species found in the area is Beach Morning Glory (*C. soldanella*), which has smaller pink flowers and kidney-shaped leaves.

Toothwort
Cardamine nuttallii (formerly *C. pulcherrima*)

MUSTARD FAMILY

This plant is a perennial that grows from a short rhizome in moist deciduous woods. The basal leaves are long-stalked, round to heart-shaped, with shallowly rounded teeth. The stem leaves are few, grouped mostly above the middle of the stem, and are compound with three lance-shaped leaflets. The inflorescence is several few-flowered racemes on erect to ascending stems. The individual flowers are white, four-petalled, cruciform, with dark pencilling on the petals.

The genus name, *Cardamine*, is derived from the Greek *kardamis*, which is the name given to an Old World species of Cress. The specific name honours 19th-century English botanist and ornithologist Thomas Nuttall, curator of the Harvard Botanic Gardens and author of *Genera of North American Plants*. The common name originates from the resemblance of the white, rounded rhizomes of the plant to teeth, *wort* being an Old English name for "plant." The plant also goes by the locally common names Beautiful Bitter Cress, Nuttall's Toothwort, and Slender Toothwort.

Stinging Nettle
Urtica dioica

NETTLE FAMILY

This plant occurs in moist mountain forests, thickets, and meadows at various elevations. The plant has a square stem and can grow to 2 m tall. The leaves are narrowly lance-shaped, opposite, simple, toothed, and appear wrinkled. The leaves are shiny on top, up to 15 cm long, tapered to the tip, and covered with small hairs. The flowers are inconspicuous, green, and occur in drooping clusters from the leaf axils. Both male and female flowers appear on the same plant.

The genus name, *Urtica*, is derived from the Latin *uro*, meaning "to burn," a very understandable reference to anybody who has had the misfortune of getting involved with the stinging hairs that cover this plant. Interestingly, despite the nasty skin irritation that can result from casual contact, the leaves of the plant are considered important both as a food and as a medicine. The plant is rendered harmless when cooked. Modern herbalists value the plant as an astringent and a diuretic. Native peoples often used the stems of mature plants for making string and other cordage material.

Alaska Rein-Orchid
Piperia unalascensis

ORCHID FAMILY

Virginia Skilton image

This orchid grows up to 90 cm tall from an egg-shaped tuber at low to middle elevations in dry to moist forests and open, rocky, dry slopes. The plant has two to five lance-shaped basal leaves that are up to 15 cm long and 4 cm wide, which usually wither prior to the flowers blooming. The inflorescence is a spike-like spirally arranged raceme at the top of the stem. The small flowers are greenish to white, moderately fragrant, and have a triangular lip with a spur of about equal size.

The genus name, *Piperia*, honours Charles Vancouver Piper, an early 20th-century Canadian-born agronomist and botanist who worked for the United States Department of Agriculture. The species name, *unalascensis*, refers to the Aleutian Island Unalaska, where the plant was first found. The plant also goes by the locally common name of Slender-Spire Orchid. Elegant Rein-Orchid (*P. elegans*) is a similar species that occurs in similar habitat. It has a spur that is about twice as long as the lip.

Heart-Leaved Twayblade
Listera cordata

ORCHID FAMILY

This small orchid, standing about 20 cm tall, prefers a cool, damp, mossy habitat. As a consequence of its size and preferred location, it is an easy flower to miss. The white flowers are scattered up the stem in an open raceme. The lip of the flower in this species is deeply split, almost in two. The stem leaf structure of the genus is distinctive, with two leaves appearing opposite to each other part way up the stem.

The common name, Twayblade, refers to the two stem leaves. The genus name, *Listera*, commemorates Dr. Martin Lister, an English naturalist of the 1600s. The species name, *cordata*, means "heart-shaped," a reference to the shape of the stem leaves. Several other Twayblades appear in the same habitat. All are relatively rare, and they all have two leaves held flat and opposite about halfway up the stem. Northwest Twayblade (*L. caurina*) has larger leaves than this species, and a larger lip that is not notched at the tip.

Hooded Ladies' Tresses
Spiranthes romanzoffiana

ORCHID FAMILY

This orchid is reasonably common in swampy places, meadows, open shady woods and lakeshores and can stand up to 60 cm tall. The characteristic feature of the plant is the crowded flower spike, which can contain up to 60 densely spaced white flowers that appear to coil around the end of the stem in three spiraling ranks. When newly bloomed, the flower has a wonderful aroma, which most people say smells like vanilla.

The common name of the plant is a reference to the braid-like appearance of the flowers, similar to a braid in a lady's hair. The genus name is derived from the Greek *speira*, meaning "coil," and *anthos*, meaning "flower," referring to the spiral inflorescence. The species name honours Count Nikolai Romanzoff, a 19th-century Russian minister of state and patron of science. The species was first discovered on the Aleutian island of Unalaska, when Alaska was still a Russian territory.

Large Round-Leaved Orchid
Platanthera orbiculata (formerly *Habenaria orbiculata*)

ORCHID FAMILY

Virginia Skilton image

This plant grows in moist, mossy forests, wetlands, swamps, and bogs from low to subalpine elevations. The basal leaves are a pair of round to oblong elliptic leaves, 16 cm long and almost as wide. They lie flat on the ground, opposite or nearly so, one to the other. The flowering stem is 50 cm tall and has no leaves, just a few lance-shaped bracts. The inflorescence occurs as a loose flowering spike of 5 to 25 flowers at the top of the stem. The flowers are whitish-green, and the lower petal forms a straight, linear or strap-shaped lip about 2.5 cm long, with a long, tapering, cylindrical spur that curves upward at the tip. The spur is longer than the lip.

The origin of the genus name, *Platanthera*, is discussed in the note on One-Leaved Rein-Orchid (*P. obtusata*), shown on page 138. The species name, *orbiculata*, refers to the round shape of the leaves. The plant was first described for science by Frederick Pursh in 1814 in his *Flora Americae Septentrionalis*. The plant is pollinated by moths.

Mountain Lady's Slipper
Cypripedium montanum

ORCHID FAMILY

This distinctive and relatively rare orchid grows up to 60 cm tall, and occurs in dry to moist woods and open areas from mid- to subalpine elevations. The lower petal forms a white, pouch-shaped lower lip that has purple markings. The sepals and lateral petals are brownish, have wavy margins, and appear to spiral away from the stem. The attractive leaves are alternate, broadly elliptical, clasping on the stem, and have prominent veins. One to three flowers appear on the stem, and they are wonderfully fragrant.

The genus name, *Cypripedium*, is derived from the Greek *kupris*, meaning "Aphrodite," the Greek goddess of love and beauty, and *pedilon*, meaning "foot" or "slipper," thus Aphrodite's slipper. The species name, *montanum*, means "of the mountains." This plant is relatively rare in its natural habitat, but has been made more so by indiscriminate picking and attempts at transplantation, which virtually never are successful. The plant depends upon the flower for nutrition, and picking the flower will kill the plant. Flowers in this genus are often referred to as Moccasin Flowers.

One-Leaved Rein-Orchid
Platanthera obtusata (formerly *Habenaria obtusata*)

ORCHID FAMILY

The solitary leaf and small, greenish-white flowers of this orchid make it easy to distinguish from other local orchids. The single, basal leaf is oblong and blunt on the end, tapering to the sheathing base. The stem grows up to about 20 cm tall, with the flowers distributed up the stem. The flowers have a strap-shaped lip, and a tapering spur which is about as long as the lip.

The genus name, *Platanthera*, is Latin for "flat anthers." The former genus name, *Habenaria*, is derived from the Latin *habena*, meaning "rein," a reference to the rein-like appendages on the lip, hence the source of the common name. The species name, *obtusata* means "blunt," a reference to the shape of the single leaf. The species is pollinated by mosquitoes, which are usually in no short supply in the habitat of this lovely orchid: mossy forests, bogs, and swamps.

Western Rattlesnake Plantain
Goodyera oblongifolia

ORCHID FAMILY

This orchid grows in shaded, dry or moist coniferous woods in the mountains. It is a single-stemmed, stiff-hairy perennial that grows up to 40 cm tall. The basal leaves are distinctive, with a white, mottled midvein, and whitish lateral veins. The robust downy spike bears small greenish-white flowers in a loose, one-sided or twisted raceme, with the lower flowers blooming first. The lip of the flower has a wide-open mouth pressed up against the overhanging hood.

The common name originates from the mottled white markings on the leaves, which reminded early European settlers of the markings on a rattlesnake. Plantain comes from the Latin *planta*, meaning "foot," a reference to the broad, flat, foot-like leaves. The genus name commemorates the 17th-century English botanist John Goodyer.

White Clover (Dutch Clover)
Trifolium repens

PEA FAMILY

This common plant was introduced from Eurasia for hay, pasture, and soil improvement , as it is a nitrogen fixer in the soil. The leaves are composed of three leaflets – occasionally four if you are lucky – and creep along the ground. The flowers are white and clustered on short, slender stalks in round heads. On close examination the flower cluster is quite intricate in shape, and worthy of close examination.

The name Clover originates from the Latin *clava*, meaning the three-headed cudgel carried by Hercules. That same reference is seen in playing cards, in the suit called clubs. Historically, the flowers have been used to flavour cheese and tobacco, and have even been used in famine time to make bread.

White Sweet-Clover
Melilotus alba

PEA FAMILY

A plant of roadsides, ditches, embankments, and pastures, this introduced plant is quite common. It grows to over 2 m tall, with smooth, leafy, branched stems. The leaflets are slightly toothed, and appear in threes. The flowers are white, and appear in long, narrow, tapered clusters at the top of the plant and in the leaf axils. Each individual flower has a typical pea shape, with standard, wings, and a keel. In this flower the standard and wings are about the same length, and the wings are attached to the keel.

The genus name, *Melilotus*, is derived from the Greek *meli*, meaning "honey," and *lotos*, the name of some clover-like plant in the Mediterranean. *Alba* means "white." This plant, and a similar plant, Yellow Sweet-Clover, (*M. officinalis*), was introduced as a forage plant for livestock. Both plants contain coumarin, which imparts an overwhelmingly sweet fragrance when you are near the plants or when they are cut for hay.

Large-Flowered Collomia (Grand Collomia)
Collomia grandiflora

PHLOX FAMILY

Jim Riley image

This annual occurs in dry open woods and on grassy slopes from valley to middle elevations. The flowering stem may be solitary or branched, and stands up to 1 m tall. The leaves are narrow, alternate on the stem, lance-shaped, and smooth on the margins (entire). The stem supports a closely packed head of white to pale yellow to salmon-coloured trumpet-shaped flowers about 3 cm long. The floral tube has five gently pointed lobes. There are leafy bracts just below the flower head. The flowers bloom early and last a long time.

The genus name, *Collomia*, is derived from the Greek *kolla*, which means "glue," a reference to a sticky secretion around the seeds, particularly when they are moistened. The species name refers to the relatively large flowering head. Vari-Leaved Collomia (*C. heterophylla*) is an allied species that blooms in the region. It is a much shorter plant, standing only 40 cm tall, and it has pink or lavender flowers, usually occurring as solitaries at the stem top.

Spreading Phlox
Phlox diffusa

PHLOX FAMILY

Jim Riley image

This variable species is widespread in the region and forms colonies of up 1 m square in various habitats from semi-deserts to mountain screes and rocky areas. The colour of the flowers varies considerably, even in the same colonies, and can be white, to pink, to various shades of purple, lavender and violet. The plant is a mat-forming perennial with linear, opposite, often sharply pointed leaves that are fused at the base in pairs. The five-lobed flowers may have narrow lobes, like the spokes in a wheel, or they may be wider and even overlapping. The saucer-like flowers occur at the branch ends.

The genus name, *Phlox*, is Greek for "flame," descriptive of the colours of the flowers. The species name, *diffusa*, means "spreading loosely." This flower often blooms early in the spring and adds a wonderful spectrum of colour to an otherwise drab landscape. It is a popular species in rock gardens.

Mouse-Ear Chickweed (Field Chickweed)
Cerastium arvense

PINK FAMILY

This early-blooming plant thrives in dry grasslands and rocky and disturbed ground, often forming large mats of white flowers in the spring. The white flowers appear in loose clusters, often many flowers to each plant. The five white petals are notched and have green lines on them as nectar guides for insects.

The upper part of the leaf resembles a mouse's ear, thus the common name for the plant. The genus name, *Cerastium*, is derived from the Greek *keras*, meaning "horn," a reference to the shape of the seed capsule. The species name, *arvense*, means "of cultivated fields."

Sweet-Flowered Androsace (Rock Jasmine)
Androsace chamaejasme

PRIMROSE FAMILY

This striking, low-growing cushion plant is seldom more than 10 cm tall but can form mats of flowers on rocky ledges and fields. The flowers are borne on a single, white-hairy stem, and they occur in umbels of four or five flowers. The petals of the flowers are white, with a yellow or orange eye. Though small, these flowers have a wonderful aroma that is worth getting down on hands and knees to smell.

The genus name, *Androsace*, is derived from the Greek *androsakes*, a marine plant. The species name, *chamaejasme*, is from the Greek *chamai*, meaning "low on the ground," and *jasme*, meaning "jasmine," thus a common name for the plant: Rock Jasmine.

Western Starflower (Broad-Leaved Starflower)
Trientalis latifolia

PRIMROSE FAMILY

This plant appears at low to middle elevations in shady, moist forests, forest openings, and seepage sites. The small pink to white saucer-shaped corolla is deeply divided into six or seven sharply pointed lobes. Each flower is borne on a thin curved stalk that rises from the centre of the leaf whorl. The leaves are oval elliptic and grow in a whorl at the top of a stem that grows low to the ground. The fruits are round white cases that resemble tiny soccer balls.

The genus name, *Trientalis*, is Latin for "one third of a foot," which aptly describes the height of the plant. The common name, Starflower, has been applied because the flowers grow on a very slender stalk, leaving them apparently hanging in the air like tiny stars.

Columbia Lewisia
Lewisia columbiana

PURSLANE FAMILY

Doug Skilton image

This plant has a large, branched, fleshy root from which springs several erect, branched stems that stand 30 cm tall. The basal leaves are numerous, linear to narrowly spoon-shaped, and up to 10 cm long. The stem leaves are alternate and 3 cm long, reducing in size up the stem. The inflorescence occurs in an open, branched panicle with many flowers on short stems. The individual flowers have seven to nine white, egg-shaped petals that are veined in pink to rose. The petal tips are notched. The plant grows in rocky outcrops and gravelly slopes at middle to high elevations.

The genus name, *Lewisia*, honours Captain Meriwether Lewis of the Lewis and Clark Expedition, 1804–1806. Lewis and Clark were not trained botanists but they were keen observers and collected an impressive number of plant specimens during their journey, many of which were successfully sent back to Philadelphia for scientific inspection. Deservedly, many North American plants have been named for Lewis, and the journals kept by the expedition are priceless artifacts. The specific name, *columbiana*, means "of western North America."

Miner's Lettuce
Claytonia perfoliata (also *Montia perfoliata*)

PURSLANE FAMILY

This plant is a succulent annual that grows from a taproot, putting up several ascending to upright stems up to 30 cm tall in vernally moist, shady forests, thickets and meadows at low to moderate elevations. The species is quite variable in size, colour and shape of its leaves. The basal leaves are spreading to erect, elliptic and abruptly tapered to the stalk. The stem leaves are paired, opposite and fused on both margins around the stem, forming a disc. The stem appears to perforate the disc, the source of the specific name, *perfoliata*. The inflorescence consists of whorled racemes of five-petalled flowers which are short-stalked or stalkless, arising from the centre of the disc.

The genera *Claytonia* and *Montia* appear to be synonyms in today's taxonomy, though they were once looked upon as allied but separate. *Claytonia* honours 17th-century English botanist John Clayton, who collected plants in the Virginia area. *Montia* honours 18th-century Italian botanist Giuseppe Monti. A number of the plants in the genera are locally known as Spring Beauty and Miner's Lettuce. The latter name arises because early miners and pioneers ate the leaves of the plants as greens. Several allied plants appear in similar habitat. Siberian Lettuce (*C. sibirica*), shown on page 149, has similar flowers, but its opposite, paired stem leaves are not fused as in this species. Red-Stemmed Miner's Lettuce (*C. rubra*), has fused uppermost leaves, red stems and small, white flowers appearing on short stems; Small-Leaved Montia (*C. parvifolia*), has alternate stem leaves and a short raceme of pink flowers.

Siberian Lettuce
Claytonia sibirica (also *Montia sibirica*)

PURSLANE FAMILY

This plant is sprawling to erect, grows from a slender taproot or rhizome, and appears on moist stream banks, meadows, beaches, thickets, and low-elevation forests. The basal leaves are numerous, long-stalked, and egg-shaped to triangular. The stem leaves are opposite, paired, sessile, and egg-shaped, but are not fused together. The flowers appear in a terminal open cluster of up to three flowers on stalks 5 cm long. Each white to pink flower has five dark-veined, notched petals and a distinctive small bract at its base.

The origin of the genus names, *Claytonia* and *Montia*, are explained in the note on Miner's Lettuce (*C. perfoliata*), shown on page 148. A number of the plants in the genera are locally known as Spring Beauty and Miner's Lettuce. This plant is also known by the locally common names Siberian Miner's Lettuce, Siberian Spring Beauty, and Candy Flower. Native peoples made extensive medicinal use of the plant for a variety of ailments.

Western Spring Beauty
Claytonia lanceolata

PURSLANE FAMILY

The flowers of this early-blooming plant are white, but may appear pink, owing to the reddish veins in the petals, and the pink anthers. The tips of the petals are distinctly notched. The plants are usually less than 20 cm tall, and the flowers appear in loose, terminal, short-stalked clusters. The plant grows from a small, white, edible corm.

The origin of the genus names, *Claytonia* and *Montia*, are explained in the note on Miner's Lettuce (*C. perfoliata*), shown on page 148. Western Spring Beauty is in the same family as the Bitterroot (*Lewisia rediviva*), and like the Bitterroot, was used by Native peoples as food. In fact, another locally common name for the plant is Indian Potato, it being said that the corms of the plant taste like potatoes. Bears and rodents also make use of the corms of the plant for food. Ungulates often eat the flowers and leaves. Alpine Spring Beauty (*C. megarhiza*) is a relatively rare but similar plant that occurs in the alpine zone of the Rocky Mountains. It has spoon-shaped, reddish-green basal leaves, and grows from a fleshy, swollen taproot.

Creeping Raspberry (Five-Leaved Bramble)
Rubus pedatus

ROSE FAMILY

This ubiquitous low-growing plant spreads by runners (stolons) up to 1 m long, which root at the nodes and produce short, erect flowering stems that have no prickles. The leaves are alternate, coarsely double-toothed, long-stalked, and palmately compound, with three to five leaflets. The flowers are solitary on a long, slender stalk. They are white, with five spreading petals. The fruits are one to six red, juicy, tasty drupelets that make up a more or less coherent cluster which is the raspberry.

The origin of the genus name, *Rubus*, is explained in the note on Dwarf Raspberry (*R. arcticus*), shown on page 58. The species name, *pedatus*, is derived from the Latin *pedata*, which means "like a bird's foot," a reference to the leaf structure of the plant. The fruits of the plant are used as food by birds and mammals, including humans. The plant also goes by the locally common names Strawberryleaf Raspberry and Five-Leaved Bramble.

Himalayan Blackberry
Rubus discolor

ROSE FAMILY

As might be indicated by the common name, this plant is an immigrant that has become a noxious weed in North America, taking over roadsides, laneways and disturbed areas. The plant is a coarse shrub that grows up to 5 m tall. It is very invasive, forming impenetrable thickets with its erect to ascending, arching, sprawling, trailing branches. The plant is also very well armed with thorns. The leaves are evergreen, alternate, palmately compound, usually with three leaflets, double-saw-toothed and abruptly sharp-pointed at the tip. The flowers are white to pinkish, with five spreading petals, and they occur in open clusters of 5 to 20 at branch ends. The fruits are smooth, black, globe-like, coherent clusters of drupelets.

The origin of the genus name, *Rubus*, is explained in the note on Dwarf Raspberry (*R. arcticus*), shown on page 58. The species name, *discolor*, most probably arises from the Latin *color*, or colour, with the prefix *dis*, in this case meaning "negation," ergo "no colour," or white, a reference to the flowers. The fruits of the plant are used as food by birds and mammals, including humans. At one time, my eldest son had a very large blackberry infestation on his property in Washington State. He introduced goats to the environment, and over time they devoured almost all of the brambles, while at the same time expanding their enclosure considerably.

Indian Plum (Osoberry)
Oemleria cerasiformis

ROSE FAMILY

Kevin Newell image

This deciduous shrub or small tree is erect and loosely branched, and grows up to 4 m tall in dry to moist open woods and along stream banks at low elevations. The leaves are lance-shaped and up to 12 cm long, fuzzy, green above and grey-green below, often occurring in clumps attached at the same point on the stem. The leaves emit a scent of cucumber when crushed. The plant is dioecious, with male and female flowers appearing on separate plants. The male flowers are said to have an objectionable odour; the female flowers less so. The flowers appear from the leaf axils early in the spring in drooping racemes of bell-shaped white flowers. Individual flowers have five greenish white petals. The flowers precede or coincide with the emergence of the leaves. The fruits are drupes about 1 cm long borne on red stems. They are orange when young, and blue-black at maturity.

The genus name, *Oemleria*, honours 18th-century German naturalist Augustus Gottlieb Oemler. The species name, *cerasiformis*, means "cherry-like," though there seems to be some dispute among the authorities as to whether the reference is to the fruits or the leaves of the plant. The fruits are said to be very bitter, but are apparently relished by birds and mammals, both large and small. The common name, Osoberry, is thought to arise from a Native word, *oso*, which means "bear," a reference to bears eating the fruits of the plant. Some Native peoples ate the fruits, and they also used the twigs and bark in poultices and making tea.

Ocean Spray (Cream Bush)
Holodiscus discolor

ROSE FAMILY

This is an erect, loosely branched deciduous shrub that grows to over 3 m tall on coastal bluffs and in dry to moist woods. The leaves are ovate, up to 8 cm long, lobed, toothed, and woolly-hairy underneath. The flowers are large pyramidal clusters of tiny white flowers that occur at the branch ends. The plant is aptly named. The clusters of white flowers bring to mind the foam cast about by crashing waves and ocean winds. The plant has a sweet scent from a distance, but is said to be musty smelling in close proximity.

The genus name, *Holodiscus*, is derived from the Greek *holo*, which means "whole," and *discus*, which means "disk," a reference to the placement of the flower parts. The species name, *discolor*, is derived from the Latin *dis*, which in this context means "two," most probably a reference to the fact that the white flowers turn brown as they wither. The wood of the plant is exceptionally hard and strong. Native peoples used it to fashion a number of tools, including arrows, harpoons, digging implements, anchor pins for tepees, awls, etc. The wood does not burn readily, so it was also used for the manufacture of cooking tools and spits for roasting salmon.

Pacific Ninebark
Physocarpus capitatus

ROSE FAMILY

This is an erect to spreading, deciduous shrub that grows to 4 m tall in streamside thickets, moist woods, and lake margins at low to middle elevations. The bark is brown and shredding. The leaves are dark green above, lighter below, alternate, three- to five-lobed, toothed, and conspicuously veined. The flowers are small and white, with five petals and numerous stamens, and they occur in rounded clusters at the ends of the branches. The fruits are reddish bunches of dried, inflated follicles.

The genus name, *Physocarpus*, is derived from the Greek *phusa*, which means "bellows" or "bladder," a reference to the inflated fruits, and *karpos*, fruit. The genus name, *capitatus*, is a reference to the way the flowers form a head-like cluster. Native peoples used the wood of the plant extensively for the manufacture of tools. Some tribes used the bark to make concoctions for medicinal purposes. The common name Ninebark arises because it was believed the plant has nine layers of shredding bark.

Partridgefoot (Creeping Spiraea)
Luetkea pectinata

ROSE FAMILY

This dwarf evergreen shrub creates extensive mats as it creeps over the ground in moist meadows, scree slopes, and shady areas near timberline. It often grows where snow melts late in the season. The leaves are mainly basal, numerous, smooth, fan-shaped, and much divided. Old leaves wither and persist for long periods of time. The white to cream-coloured flowers appear in short, crowded clusters atop erect stems. The flowers have four to six pistils, and about 20 stamens, which are conspicuous on the flowers.

The genus name, *Luetkea*, honours Count F.P. Lütke, a 19th-century Russian sea captain and explorer. This is the only species in the genus. The species name, *pectinata*, means "with narrow divisions – like the teeth of a comb," and is a reference to the structure of the leaves. The common name, Partridgefoot, is derived from the supposed resemblance between the leaves of the species and the footprint of a partridge. Given the subalpine and alpine habitat of this plant, it might be more appropriately called Ptarmiganfoot.

Sticky Cinquefoil
Potentilla glandulosa

ROSE FAMILY

This plant inhabits open forests and meadows at low to middle elevations. It grows to about 40 cm tall from a branched rootstock, and the leaves and stems are covered with glandular hairs that exude a sticky, aromatic fluid. The leaves are mainly basal and pinnately divided into five to nine sharply toothed oval leaflets. The flowers are typical of the *Potentillas* and are pale yellow to creamy white, occurring in small open clusters at the top of the stems.

The origin of the genus name, *Potentilla*, is explained in the note on Silverweed (*P. anserina*), shown on page 266. The species name, *glandulosa*, is a reference to the glandular hairs that cover the plant. This plant, like other members of the family, has high tannin content and is used as an astringent and anti-inflammatory. Sulphur Cinquefoil (*P. recta*), is a related species that occurs in similar habitat. It is an invasive weed introduced from Eurasia. It grows up to 80 cm tall and has mostly stem leaves that are palmately divided into five to seven deeply toothed leaflets, with pale yellow flowers that are in a flat-topped cluster at the top of the stem.

Thimbleberry
Rubus parviflorus

ROSE FAMILY

This is a plant that often forms thickets on avalanche slopes and at the margins of forests and streams. The plant is closely related to the raspberry, but this vigorous shrub does not have prickles or spines. The plant can grow up to 2 m tall. It has large leaves, each with three to five lobes, with jagged-toothed margins, resembling a maple leaf in shape. The flowers are white, with a central core of yellow stamens. There are usually three to five flowers in clusters at the ends of branches. The bright red fruit looks like a flattened raspberry but it is rather tasteless and very seedy.

The origin of the genus name, *Rubus*, is explained in the note on Dwarf Raspberry (*R. arcticus*), shown on page 58. The specific name, *parviflorus*, is derived from Greek *parvus*, which means "small," and the Latin *flora*, which means "flower," ergo, small-flowered. The name is puzzling given that Thimbleberry flowers are not at all small in the scheme of things. Native peoples peeled the young shoots of Thimbleberry and ate them raw, or cooked them with meat in stews. The large leaves were widely used as temporary containers, to line baskets, and to separate items in the same basket. They also make a good biodegradable toilet tissue substitute when needed.

Trailing Blackberry
Rubus ursinus

ROSE FAMILY

This low-growing, sprawling and trailing shrub will grow up to 5 m long as it spreads along the ground, usually in moist, shady places, along streams, in logged areas, and along lakeshores. It is armed with slender, straight to slightly recurved thorns that can be quite nasty when encountered. The leaves are deciduous, alternate, pinnately compound with three leaflets, broadly egg-shaped, and doubly saw-toothed. The flowers are white with five spreading petals, and they appear in small, open, flat-topped clusters above the leaves. The fruits are smooth, black, globe-like, coherent clusters of drupelets.

The origin of the genus name, *Rubus*, is explained in the note on Dwarf Raspberry (*R. arcticus*), shown on page 58. The species name, *ursinus*, is derived from the Latin *ursus*, which means "bear," the reference most probably being to the northern-hemisphere constellation Great Bear (Ursa Major), that being where the plant occurs. The plant is dioecious, which means that the male and female flowers are found on different plants. Only the female flowers (pistillate) produce fruits. The fruits of the plant are used as food by birds and mammals, including humans. The plant is also known by the locally common name California Blackberry. Creeping Raspberry (*R. pedatus*), shown on page 151, is an allied plant that occurs in the region. It has similar flowers, but is an unarmed plant – without thorns or prickles.

Western Mountain Ash
Sorbus scopulina

ROSE FAMILY

This deciduous, erect to spreading shrub grows to 4 m tall in moist open or shaded places from the foothills to the subalpine zones. The branches are slightly white-hairy and sticky when new; reddish-grey to yellowish when mature. The leaves are alternate and pinnately compound – leaflets appearing opposite each other on both sides of a common axis – with 11 to 13 leaflets per leaf. The leaflets are sharply tipped and sharply toothed from tip to base. The flowers are white and saucer-shaped, with five broad petals, and they occur in large flat-topped clusters. The fruits are glossy orange to red berry-like pomes in dense clusters.

The origin of the genus name, *Sorbus*, is a matter of some contention. It was either the Latin name for mountain ash, or was the Greek name for oak, depending on which authority you choose to follow. The species name, *scopulina*, means "growing in rocky places." Some Native peoples ate the pomes of this plant, but most looked upon them as inedible. Some tribes boiled the peeled branches or inner bark of the plant to make medicinal concoctions. The plant is used quite extensively as a garden ornamental. The fruit clusters are a favoured food of a variety of bird species.

White Dryad (White Mountain Avens)
Dryas octopetala

ROSE FAMILY

This dwarf evergreen grows close to the ground, forming mats on gravelly soil in the alpine zone. The leaves are oblong to lance-shaped, leathery, dark green, with edges that are scalloped and often rolled under. The creamy-coloured flowers bloom in abundance soon after snows melt. The flowers are borne on short, hairy, leafless stems that rise from the mats of leaves. Each flower has eight petals, thus the species name *octopetala*. The fruits are similar to those of the Drummond's Mountain Avens (*D. drummondii*), shown on page 263.

The genus is named after Dryas, the wood nymph in Greek mythology. This plant is superbly adapted to its harsh natural environment. The plant has root nodules that store nitrogen in a nutrient-poor habitat. White Dryad is also valued by rock gardeners as a ground cover.

Wild Strawberry
Fragaria virginiana

ROSE FAMILY

This is a plant of shaded to open gravelly soils and thickets from prairie to alpine habitats. The single five-petalled white flower appears on a leafless stem that is usually shorter than the leaves are long. The stamens are numerous and yellow. The leaves are rounded to broadly oval, toothed, with three leaflets on short stalks. The fruit is a red berry covered with sunken, seed-like achenes. New plants are often established from reddish runners.

Strawberry is said to come from the Anglo-Saxon name *streowberie* because the runners from the plant are strewn across the ground. The genus name, *Fragaria*, means "fragrance." Strawberry plants are rich in iron, calcium, potassium, sodium, and vitamin C. The fruits are delicious, with a more pronounced flavour than domestic strawberries. The leaves have been used to make tea, and have also been used for medicinal purposes.

Alaska Saxifrage (Rusty Saxifrage)
Saxifraga ferruginea

SAXIFRAGE FAMILY

This plant grows in moist soils, on rocky outcrops, and along spring banks in the subalpine and alpine zones. The leaves are basal only, hairy, and wedge-shaped with toothed margins. The numerous white flowers bloom in an open inflorescence on hairy stems. The flowers have five petals. The three upper petals are broader than the lower two petals, have yellow spots, and abruptly narrow at the base. Some of the flowers on the plant may become leafy bulblets and drop off the plant.

The origin of the genus name, *Saxifraga*, is explained in the note on Purple Saxifrage (*S. oppositifolia*), shown on page 219. The species name, *ferruginea*, is derived from the Latin *ferrum*, which means "iron," a reference to the rusty colour of the calyx. That rusty colour gives rise to another common name, Rusty Saxifrage.

Bishop's Cap (Bare-Stemmed Mitrewort)
Mitella nuda

SAXIFRAGE FAMILY

This wonderful plant occurs in moist to dry forests, bogs, thickets, and along streams, from the montane to the subalpine elevations, particularly in the eastern part of the region. The plant stands erect and grows up to 20 cm tall. The leaves are basal, heart to kidney-shaped, and short-lobed, with rounded teeth. The flowers are tiny, and occur in an open cluster, scattered up the leafless stem. The saucer-shaped flowers are very distinctive, and when examined closely they are reminiscent of some kind of a satellite dish such as might be found in outer space, complete with antennae festooned around the circumference of the flower.

The genus name, *Mitella*, is derived from the Greek *mitra*, which means "a cap," a reference to the flower's resemblance to a mitre – the hat worn by bishops – ergo the common name Bishop's Cap. The species name, *nuda*, means "naked," most probably a reference to the leafless stem of the plant. Plants in the genus are usually referred to as Mitreworts. There are a number of Mitreworts in the region, differing in detail from this species, but all members of the genus exhibit the distinctive flower arrangement displayed by this species. A full catalogue of the various Mitreworts is outside the ambit of this book and specific identification may require further research. These plants are certainly among the most fascinating in the forest.

Early Saxifrage
Saxifraga integrifolia

SAXIFRAGE FAMILY

This is a plant of wet to dry meadows and grassy slopes that grows from short rhizomes or bulblets. It has a single, leafless, glandular-hairy flowering stem that grows to 30 cm tall. The basal leaves are long-stalked, egg-shaped, up to 7 cm long and half as wide, covered with red or purple glandular hairs, and often have rusty, tangled hairs on the underside. The inflorescence is a cluster of conical, open-branched, white or yellowish flowers which have egg-shaped petals and rusty hairs. There is a leafy, rusty-woolly bract beneath the inflorescence.

The origin of the genus name, *Saxifraga*, is discussed in the note on Purple Saxifrage. (*S. oppositifolia*), shown on page 219. The species name, *integrifolia*, means that the leaf margins are entire, i.e., smooth and not toothed. The plant is also known by the locally common names of Grassland Saxifrage and Wholeleaf Saxifrage

Foamflower (False Mitrewort)
Tiarella trifoliate var. *laciniata*

SAXIFRAGE FAMILY

These beautiful flowers inhabit moist coniferous woods, stream banks and trails from low to subalpine elevations. The plant grows up to 50 cm tall, and the flowers are white or pinkish, arranged in open panicles well above the leaves. The leaves are compound, usually with three leaflets. The middle leaflet is usually three-lobed and toothed.

The genus name, *Tiarella*, is derived from the Latin *tiara*, an ancient Persian, turban-like headdress. The species name, *trifoliata*, refers to the compound leaf with three leaflets. Other common names applied to the plant are Laceflower and False Mitrewort.

Fringe Cup
Tellima grandiflora

SAXIFRAGE FAMILY

This plant grows from scaly rhizomes in moist woods, along streams and in avalanche chutes at low to middle elevations. The long-stalked basal leaves are heart-shaped, 8 cm wide and about as long, irregularly toothed, scalloped on the margin and covered with white hairs. The flowering stems stand 80 cm tall and the flowers occur in a one-sided spike-like terminal cluster of 10–35 nodding blooms. The individual flowers have five greenish-white petals that are fringed at the tips. The flowers usually turn pinkish or reddish with age.

The genus name, *Tellima*, is an anagram for *Mitella*, a genus within the Saxifrage Family, the plants of which are generally referred to as Mitreworts. The species name, *grandiflora*, means "large flowered," which is puzzling given that the flowers of Fringe Cup are only 1–1.5 cm long.

Leather-Leaved Saxifrage
Leptarrhena pyrolifolia

SAXIFRAGE FAMILY

This plant occurs in wet, open forests, wet meadows, along streams, and in seeps in the subalpine and alpine zones. The leaves are mostly basal, oval to oblong, leathery, prominently veined, and have toothed edges. The purplish stems are erect, up to 40 cm tall, and have only one to three small leaves. The flowers are small and white, sometimes pink, and appear in tight clusters at the top of the flowering stem. Each flower has ten long stamens. The fruits of the plant are perhaps more striking than the flowers. The fruits are paired, pointed, purplish-red, single-chambered capsules in clusters atop the stem.

The genus name, *Leptarrhena*, is derived from the Greek *leptos*, which means "slender," and *arren*, which means "male," a reference to the slender stamens on the plant. The species name, *pyrolifolia*, most probably is a reference to the leaves, *Pyrola* being the genus of many Wintergreens, which have leathery leaves. This plant has been enthusiastically adopted by rock gardeners.

Spotted Saxifrage
Saxifraga bronchialis

SAXIFRAGE FAMILY

These beautiful flowers inhabit rocky crevices, rock faces, screes, and open slopes, often appearing as if by magic from the rocks. The white flowers appear in clusters at the top of the wiry brown stems, and have small red or yellow spots near the tips of the five petals. A close examination of this beautiful flower is well worth the time.

The origin of the genus name, *Saxifraga*, is explained in the note on Purple Saxifrage (*S. oppositifolia*), shown on page 219. The species name, *bronchialis*, is from the Latin *bronchus*, meaning "branch" or "division," a reference to the branching, mat-like growth of the plant. The plant is also known by the locally common name Yellow Dot Saxifrage.

Three-Toothed Mitrewort (Three-Parted Mitrewort)
Mitella trifida

SAXIFRAGE FAMILY

This grey-hairy perennial grows from a rhizome and occurs in moist forests at middle elevations. The plant is locally frequent on southern Vancouver Island and in southwestern British Columbia. The flowering stem is erect and grows up to 35 cm tall. The leaves are basal, nearly round with heart-shaped bases, long-stalked, and indistinctly lobed with five to seven lobes that may have rounded teeth on the margins. There are no leaves on the stem. The inflorescence is a spike-like cluster of 10 to 20 bell-shaped white flowers that have three elliptic lobes. The flowers are often held on one side of the hairy stem.

The origin of the genus name, *Mitella*, is explained in the narrative on Bishop's Cap (*M. nuda*), shown on page 164. The species name, *trifida*, means "cleft into three parts," a reference to the flower construction of the plant. Plants in the genus are usually referred to as Mitreworts. There are a number of Mitreworts in the region. A full catalogue of the various Mitreworts is outside the ambit of this book and specific identification may require further research. These plants are certainly among the most fascinating in the forest.

Youth-on-Age (Piggy-Back Plant)
Tolmiea menziesii

SAXIFRAGE FAMILY

This hairy, evergreen plant grows from rhizomes in moist woodlands and along streams. The long-stemmed basal leaves are heart-shaped, 3–10 cm wide and nearly as long, shallowly lobed with five to seven segments, sharply toothed, and hairy. The flowering stem grows up to 80 cm tall, and the brownish-purple flowers are distributed along the stem in erect clusters. The very interesting and distinctive thing about the plant is that it also produces new plantlets in the leaf axils – viable plants in themselves, known as gemmaceous plantlets. This is the origin of the rather peculiar common names. The plant is also known locally as Thousand Mothers for the same reason.

The genus name, *Tolmiea*, honours 19th-century Scottish physician and botanist Dr. William Fraser Tolmie. The species name, *menziesii*, honours Dr. Archibald Menzies, a physician and botanist who visited the Pacific Northwest with Captain George Vancouver's expedition of 1790–1795. The plant is said by modern authorities to cause dermatitis in some people, which is somewhat peculiar given that Native peoples are said to have used the plant for making poultices for boils.

Roundleaf Sundew
Drosera rotundifolia

SUNDEW FAMILY

Virginia Skilton image

This odd little plant lives in bogs, swamps, and fens, where it often forms colonies. It stands up to 25 cm tall and is insectivorous, meaning it eats insects, which are usually in no short supply in the plant's preferred habitat. The basal leaves are erect to ascending, have round blades on stalks up to 9 cm long, and have long reddish hairs along their margins, with each hair tipped with a sticky insect-trapping fluid. One authority describes the leaf blades as looking "like small green frying-pans." The flowers are small and white, and occur on one side only at the top of a naked flowering stem. The flowers open only in full sun. Insects are trapped in the sticky fluid on the leaves, then are digested by the plant as a source of nitrogen.

The genus name, *Drosera*, is derived from the Greek *droseros*, which means "dewy," a reference to the gland-tipped hairs on the leaves, the secretions of which make them appear moist. The species name, *rotundifolia*, refers to the leaf shape. A similar species, Narrow-Leaved Sundew (*D. anglica*) occurs in similar habitat, but its leaves are not round, and are several times longer than broad and are held upright on long stalks. *Drosera* are widespread in North America, Eurasia, and Australia.

Sitka Valerian
Valeriana sitchensis

VALERIAN FAMILY

This perennial grows up to 80 cm tall and has a somewhat succulent, squarish stem. It occurs in moist subalpine and alpine environments, in alpine meadows, and along streams. The leaves are large and opposite, divided into three to seven coarsely toothed lobes, with progressively shorter petioles up the stem. The numerous tubular flowers are crowded into a nearly flat-topped cluster at the top of the stem. The buds and young flowers are a pale lavender colour, but the flowers later fade to white. The floral tubes are notched into five equal lobes

There appear to be two schools of thought as to where this genus gets its name. One school opines that the genus name is from Valeria, a Roman province in southern Europe, now a part of Hungary. The other school contends that the genus name comes from the Latin *valere*, meaning "to be healthy," a reference to the fact that the plant has long been used for various medicinal purposes. The species name, *sitchensis*, is from Sitka Sound in southeastern Alaska, where the species was first collected and described. Two common names for the plant are Wild Heliotrope and Tobacco Root. The Tobacco Root Range in Montana takes its name from the plant. Valerian is the original source of diazepam, a tranquilizer and muscle relaxant commonly known as Valium.

Broad-Leaved Arrowhead (Wapato)
Sagittaria latifolia

WATER PLANTAIN FAMILY

Virginia Skilton image

This perennial is an aquatic plant that grows flowering stems up to 90 cm long from tubers and slender rhizomes in shallow ponds, lakeshores, marshes, slow-moving water, and ditches, from the prairies to the montane zone. The submerged leaves are simple, narrow, and tapered at both ends. The emergent leaves are distinctive. They are large (up to 25 cm long and 15 cm wide), with long stalks, and are decidedly arrowhead-shaped. The plant produces both male and female flowers, and they are different. The female flowers (pistillate) tend to develop first, and are ball-like clusters on small stalks, appearing lower on the plant than do the male flowers. The male flowers (staminate) are showy, with three broadly oval white petals, and numerous stamens. The male flowers appear on long stalks.

The genus name, *Sagittaria*, is derived from the Latin *sagitta*, which means "arrow," a reference to the shape of the emergent leaves, and the source of the common name. The species name, *latifolia*, means "broad-leaved." The tuber is described as resembling a walnut or golf ball. Wapato (sometimes spelled Wapatoo or Wappato) is the Chinook jargon trade language word for the tuber of this plant, which historically was a food and trade item. Native peoples gathered the tubers with digging sticks, or with bare toes moved around in the mud where the plants grew. Members of the Lewis and Clark Expedition ate the tubers while over-wintering on the Columbia River in 1805, and allowed that they tasted of roasted potatoes. Other common names applied to the plant include Duck Potato, Indian Potato, and Swamp Potato. Arumleaf Arrowead (*S. cuneata*) is a similar species that occurs in similar habitat in the region. It has smaller leaves, flower stalks, and flowers.

Mist Maiden (Cliff Romanzoffia)
Romanzoffia sitchensis

WATERLEAF FAMILY

Dave Ingram image

This dainty, smooth, tufted perennial is fairly rare and occurs on moist rocky cliffs and ledges only in the subalpine and alpine zones. The leaves are mostly basal, kidney-shaped, and have five to nine lobes. The white to cream-coloured flowers are borne in loose clusters on thin stems above the leaves. The flowers are five-petalled and funnel-shaped at the base, each with a yellow eye.

The genus name, *Romanzoffia*, honours Count Nikolai Romanzoff, a 19th-century Russian patron of science who sponsored scientific explorations. Hooded Ladies' Tresses (*Spiranthes romanzoffiana*), shown on page 135, is also named in his honour. The plant was first discovered in Sitka Sound, southeastern Alaska, during an expedition sponsored by Count Romanzoff, whence comes the species name.

Silverleaf Phacelia (Scorpionweed)
Phacelia hastata

WATERLEAF FAMILY

This tap-rooted perennial grows up to 50 cm tall, and occurs from low to subalpine elevations in dry basins, gravelly areas, and roadsides. The leaves are elliptic with prominent veins, and generally are covered with silvery hairs. The flowers are white to lavender, funnel-shaped, and occur in compact clusters that spiral up the stem. The flowers have five broad petal lobes, five narrow hairy sepals, and five long stamens that extend well past the petals.

The origin of the genus name, *Phacelia*, is discussed in the note on Silky Phacelia (*P. sericea*), shown on page 221. The common name, Scorpionweed, arises because some people say the coiled branches of the flower clusters resemble the tail of a scorpion. The species is called Silverleaf because of the fine, silvery hairs on the leaves. The species name, *hastata*, is derived from the Latin *hastatus*, meaning "armed with a spear," a reference to the spearhead shape of some of the leaves.

Slender Waterleaf
Hydrophyllum tenuipes

WATERLEAF FAMILY

Jim Riley image

This plant occurs in moist forests at low to moderate elevations. The leaves are large, mostly basal, sharply toothed, long-stalked, hairy, and palmately divided into five to seven pointed leaflets. The inflorescence is rounded clusters of 15 to 50 small, funnel-shaped, greenish-white to pale purple flowers. Individual flowers have five petals, with styles and stamens protruding.

The genus name, *Hydrophyllum*, translates directly from the Greek to the common name: *hydro*, which means "water," and *phyllon*, which means "leaf," most probably a reference to the wet habitat favoured by members of the genus. The species name, *tenuipes*, is from the Latin *tenuis*, meaning "slender," and *pes*, meaning "foot," hence "slender-footed." The plant also goes by the locally common name of Pacific Waterleaf. Several members of the genus occur in the region. Dwarf Waterleaf (*H. capitatum*), also known as Ballhead Waterleaf, is a small species that occurs in open woods from low to middle elevations, and has blue to white flowers in rounded clusters resembling pincushions.

Wood Sorrel
Oxalis oregana

WOOD SORREL FAMILY

This plant grows from a scaly rhizome and spreads as ground cover over the forest floor. The numerous leaves are all basal, hairy, long-stalked, notched at the tip, and clover-like, with three leaflets that are broadly heart-shaped and folded toward each other. The flowers are solitary on short, erect stems, with white to pinkish petals that are dark-veined in red or purple.

The genus name, *Oxalis*, is derived from the Greek *oxus*, which means "sour," a reference to the pleasantly sour taste of the leaves and stems. The species name, *oregana*, is a reference to the old Hudson's Bay Company territory called Oregon, which included the present-day States of Oregon and Washington. This plant also goes by the locally common name of Redwood Sorrel. Two other members of the genus occur in the region: Great Oxalis (*O. trillifolia*), which bears two to seven similar flowers in a raceme, and Yellow Wood Sorrel (*O. stricta*), which has small yellow flowers.

Blue and Purple Flowers

This section includes flowers that are predominantly blue or purple when encountered in the field, ranging from pale blue to deep purple, light violet to lavender. Some of the lighter colours of blue and purple might shade into pinks, so if you do not find the flower you are looking for here, check the other sections of this book.

Common Butterwort
Pinguicula vulgaris

BLADDERWORT FAMILY

This small plant is one of only a few carnivorous plants in the area. It grows from fibrous roots in bogs, seeps, wetlands, stream banks, and lakeshores, from valleys to the subalpine zone. The pale green to yellowish leaves are basal, short-stalked, somewhat overlapping, curled in at the margins, and form a rosette on the ground. The leaves have glandular hairs on their upper surface that exude a sticky substance which attracts and ensnares small insects. The insects are then digested by the plant, enabling it to obtain nitrogen and other nutrients. The flower is pale to dark purple, solitary, and occurs atop a leafless stem.

The common name, Butterwort, is said to come from the buttery feel of the leaves, *wort* being an Old English word that means "herb" or "a plant." The genus name, *Pinguicula*, is the diminutive of the Latin word *pinguis*, which means "fat," also a reference to the soft, greasy-feeling leaves of the plant.

Forget-Me-Not
Myosotis laxa

BORAGE FAMILY

This beautiful little flower is easily recognized by its wheel-shaped blue corolla and its prominent yellow eye. The stems are hairy and slender, and weak enough for the plant to often be decumbent (lying on the ground). The lower leaves are oblong to lance-shaped, and the middle to upper leaves are more elliptic. The flowers appear in a cluster at the top of flowering stems. The blue petals are fused at the base into a tube that spreads flat at the top. This plant occurs at lower elevations in moist habitats, but has an allied plant in the alpine community. Alpine Forget-Me-Not (*M. alpestris*) is very similar in appearance, though smaller. Forget-Me-Not frequently escapes from gardens.

The genus name, *Myosotis*, is derived from the Greek *mus*, meaning "mouse," and *ous*, meaning "ear," descriptive of the short, furred leaves of some species. The species name, *laxa*, means "open" or "loose," probably a reference to the sprawling growth habit of the plant. There seems to be some dispute as to the origin of the common name. One school of thought holds that the name dates back to the 1500s when tradition held that a blue flower was worn to retain a lover's affections. Another school of thought holds that a couple was walking along the Danube River and the woman remarked on the beauty of some blue flowers blooming on a steep slope by the river. The man attempted to fetch the flowers for his sweetheart, but fell into the river, asking her as he fell to "forget me not."

One-Flowered Cancer Root (Naked Broomrape)
Orobanche uniflora

BROOMRAPE FAMILY

This plant is a saprophyte that gets its nourishment from decaying organic matter in the soil. It has no leaves, only scaly, whitish-tan bracts on the stem. The flower is solitary at the top of an unbranched 10 cm tall stem, tube-shaped, and violet to pale purple. The flower head is 2.5 cm long, and has five lobes of relatively equal size, each with three thin, dark stripes. Bright yellow-orange anthers are seen inside the throat of the flower. The plant grows at low to middle elevations, often in clumps.

The genus name, *Orobanche,* is derived from the Greek *orobos,* which means "a clinging plant," and *ancho,* which means "to strangle," a reference to the parasitic nature of the plant. The species name, *uniflora,* indicates only one flower per stem. The plant is also known by the locally common names of Naked Broomrape and One-Flowered Broomrape. These common names arise because Scotch Broom (*Cytisus scoparius*), shown on page 261, is often the host plant in Europe. In the Pacific Northwest, the host plants are more usually those in the Stonecrop, Saxifrage and Composite Families. A related species, Clustered Cancer Root (*O. grayana*), also occurs in similar habitat, but its inflorescence is a crowded cluster of up to thirty flowers.

Menzies' Larkspur
Delphinium menziesii

BUTTERCUP FAMILY

This is the most common of the coastal Larkspurs, appearing in grassy meadows and on rocky bluffs. It is an upright perennial with hairy stems that grows to 60 cm tall. The leaves are round and deeply dissected two to three times. The distinctive flowers are highly modified, with the upper sepal forming a large, hollow, nectar-producing spur. The sepals are deep blue to purple. The petals are veined and have wavy margins. The upper two petals are often white. The flowers bloom up the stem in a loose, elongated cluster.

The genus name, *Delphinium*, is derived from the Greek *delphini*, which means "dolphin," a reference to the perceived resemblance between the plant's nectary and old drawings of dolphins. This name has been applied to plants in this genus since at least the 1st century. The species name honours 18th-century Scottish physician and botanist Archibald Menzies, who accompanied Captain George Vancouver on some of his explorations to the Pacific Northwest. The common name originated because the spur on the flower was thought to resemble the spur on the foot of a lark. All *Delphiniums* contain alkaloids, delphinine being chief among them, that are poisonous to cattle. Interestingly, sheep do not appear to be affected by the alkaloids, so sheep have often been used to eradicate the plants from pastures.

Monkshood
Aconitum columbianum

BUTTERCUP FAMILY

A plant of moist mixed coniferous forests and meadows, Monkshood has a distinctive flower construction that is unmistakable. The dark blue to purple flowers appear in terminal, open clusters, and the sepals form a hood, like those worn by monks. The leaves are large, long-stalked, alternate and shaped like large maple leaves.

The genus name, *Aconitum*, is derived from the Greek *acon*, meaning "dart," a reference to the fact that arrows were often tipped with poison from this plant, the entire plant being poisonous. The plant contains alkaloids that can cause paralysis, decreased blood pressure and temperature, and can cause death within a few hours. The plant is also known by the locally common name Columbian Monkshood.

Blue Sailors (Chicory)
Cichorium intybus

COMPOSITE FAMILY

This native of Eurasia grows up to 1.75 m tall at low elevations on dry plateaus, fields, grasslands and waste areas. The basal leaves are lance-shaped and strongly toothed to lobed. The flowers have sky blue ray flowers and no disk flowers, and they occur singly or in small groups widely spaced along the long branches, arising from the bases of the stem leaves. The flowers open only in the daylight. The stems exude a bitter-tasting, milky juice when broken.

The common name, Chicory, and the genus name are derived from the original Arabic name for wild chicory. The plant has long been used as food, and is known as Belgium Endive in the commercial vegetable trade. The leaves of this plant are eaten as a salad green, a practice dating back to the ancient Egyptians, and the roots are roasted and ground as a coffee substitute. The species name, *intybus*, is Latin meaning "endive." The common name, Blue Sailors, is said to originate in a legend about a young woman who fell madly in love with a sailor. The sailor left her for his real love – the sea – and the woman was heart-broken and pitifully lonely. The gods took pity on her and changed her into a beautiful blue flower, thus Blue Sailors.

Cornflower (Bachelor's Button)
Centaurea cyanus

COMPOSITE FAMILY

This annual plant was introduced from the Mediterranean region as a garden ornamental, but it has escaped the garden and now inhabits dry roadsides and open, dry areas at low to middle elevations in the region. The stems are erect, branched, loosely hairy, and up to 1 m tall. The basal leaves are linear to lance-shaped, entire, white woolly below, and up to 13 cm long. The stem leaves are smaller and narrow. The plant has one to several flower heads at the ends of the ascending branches. The flowers are made up of a few large, spreading ray flowers surrounding a central cluster of disk flowers. The flowers are usually blue, but may be pink, white or purple.

The genus name, *Centaurea*, is said to be a reference to the centaur Chiron, who was supposed to have discovered some medicinal properties in the plant. The species name, *cyanus*, is derived from the Greek *kyanos*, an old name for a dark blue substance, possibly the blue gemstone lapis-lazuli, undoubtedly a reference to the colour of the flower. The common name Bachelor's Button arises from folklore, where it was held that young men in love were to wear blue flowers. If the flower fades quickly, it was a sign that the man's love would be unrequited, thus he would remain a bachelor. Cornflower is the national flower of Poland.

Oyster Plant (Purple Salsify)
Tragopogon porrifolius

COMPOSITE FAMILY

A plant of the grasslands, roadsides, ditches, and dry waste areas, Oyster Plant was introduced from Europe, and is also known as Purple Salsify. The flower is a large solitary, erect, purple head, surrounded by long, narrow green protruding bracts. The leaves are alternate, fleshy, and narrow, but broad and clasping at the base. The fruit is a mass of white, narrow, ribbed, beaked achenes that resembles the seed pod of a common dandelion but is significantly larger, approaching the size of a softball.

The flowers open on sunny mornings, but then close up around noon and stay closed for the rest of the day. They usually will not open on cloudy or rainy days. The common name, Oyster Plant, is a reference to the European practice of cultivating this plant for its fleshy root, which is said to taste like an oyster. The genus name, *Tragopogon* is derived from the Greek *tragos*, meaning "he-goat," and *pogon*, meaning "beard," probably a reference to the seeds resembling a goat's beard. Indeed, a very similar plant known commonly as Goat's Beard (*T. dubius*), is common and widespread east of the coastal mountains. It has a yellow flower, but otherwise is identical to Oyster Plant. The young leaves and roots from immature plants may be eaten. The leaves and stems exude a milky, latex-like juice when cut, which may be chewed like gum when hardened.

Tall Purple Fleabane
Erigeron peregrinus

COMPOSITE FAMILY

This plant grows up to 70 cm tall from a thick rootstock. It grows in the subalpine and alpine zones. The basal leaves are narrow and stemmed, while the stem leaves are smaller and stalkless. The flowers resemble daisies, with 30–80 rose- to purple-coloured ray florets, surrounding a yellow centre of disk florets. The large flowers are usually solitary, but there may be smaller flowers that appear from the axils of the upper leaves.

The origins of the common name, Fleabane, and the genus name, *Erigeron*, are discussed in the narrative on Daisy Fleabane (*E. compositus*), shown on page 84. This flower is sometimes referred to as Wandering Daisy.

Common Periwinkle
Vinca minor

DOGBANE FAMILY

This trailing evergreen perennial is an import from Eurasia that was introduced as a ground cover plant, and is now found in waste areas and along roadsides at low elevations. Its stems are long and branching, and it forms prostrate mats on the ground. The leaves are opposite, egg-shaped, and narrowed at the base. The five-petalled flowers are bluish to purple, up to 3 cm wide, and occur as solitaries atop short stems.

The genus name, *Vinca*, is derived from the Latin *vincio*, which means "to bind," a reference to the shoots of the plant. The specific name, *minor*, means "smaller" or "lesser." The plant also goes by the locally common names Myrtle, Creeping Myrtle, and Dwarf Periwinkle. A related species, Large Periwinkle (*V. major*) occurs in similar habitat, but it has larger leaves with hairy margins and similar flowers.

Alpine Speedwell (Alpine Veronica)
Veronica wormskjoldii (also *V. alpina)*

FIGWORT FAMILY

This erect perennial stands up to 30 cm tall, and occurs in moist meadows and along streams in the subalpine and alpine zones. The leaves are elliptic to egg-shaped, and occur in opposite pairs, spaced along the stem. The stems, leaves, and stalks of the flowers are covered with fine, sticky hairs. The flowers are numerous and occur at the top of the stem. The corolla has four united blue petals, which exhibit dark veins.

The genus name, *Veronica*, honours Saint Veronica. According to the canonization, Veronica took pity on Jesus when he was carrying his cross to Golgotha (Calvary), and she used her kerchief to wipe sweat from his face. When the kerchief came back to her, it was impressed with an image of his face – the *vera iconica* or "true likeness." The sacred relic was kept in St. Peter's in the Vatican, but the name was applied to the genus to link Saint Veronica to a common flower often seen by the pious public. The species name, *wormskjoldii*, honours Morton Wormskjold, an 18th-century Danish naturalist. The common name, Speedwell, is said to come from the old English blessing or benediction "god speed," though why the name is applied to flowers of this genus is unknown.

Coast Penstemon
Penstemon serrulatus

FIGWORT FAMILY

Virginia Skilton image

This plant is erect, with several stems growing up to 70 cm tall in meadows, open woods, and along streams from low to middle elevations. The leaves are all on the stem, up to 8 cm long, ovate, opposite, unstalked, pointed at the tip, and having small teeth on the margins. The flowers are tubular, blue to purple, and occur in whorled clusters of 10 to 30 blooms at the tip of the stem. The anthers are horseshoe-shaped. The individual flowers are typical of the Penstemons (Beardtongues), with each flower having a two-lobed upper lip, a three-lobed lower lip, and a hairy sterile stamen inside the throat of the floral tube.

The origin of the genus name, *Penstemon*, and the common name, Beard-tongue, is discussed in the note on Small-Flowered Penstemon (*P. procerus*), shown on page 195. The species name, *serrulatus*, means "saw-toothed," a reference to the small teeth on the leaf margins. The plant is also known by the locally common name Serrulate Penstemon.

Davidson's Penstemon
Penstemon davidsonii

FIGWORT FAMILY

Virginia Skilton image

This plant is a low, spreading, evergreen, matted perennial that occurs on rocky ledges, broken rock, and slopes from middle to alpine elevations. The leaves are small, thick and firm, and they appear in opposite pairs on the stem. The flowers are tubular, up to 3.5 cm long, blue to purple to lavender, and appear in clusters at the stem tips. The throat of the flower is densely white-hairy.

The origin of the genus name, *Penstemon*, and the common name, Beardtongue, is discussed in the note on Small-Flowered Penstemon (*P. procerus*), shown on page 195. The species name, *davidsonii*, honours Dr. George Davidson, a 19th-century English-born American geographer and astronomer who collected plants in California while on the staff of the U.S. Coast and Geodetic Survey. This flower tends to bloom as winter snows recede, and the blooms last a long time. The species is apparently a favourite of rock gardeners.

Slender Speedwell
Veronica filiformis

FIGWORT FAMILY

This is a Eurasian import that is a very invasive, prostrate, mat-forming plant. It spreads by vegetative propagation rather than seed. If parts of the plant are chopped into bits, as is the case when it is mowed, the small pieces of the plant will take root. The small, solitary, light blue flowers are borne on thread-like stems that arise from the leaf axils. The flowers have four somewhat asymmetrical, spreading lobes, with two stamens and a single pistil that is clubbed at the top.

The origin of the genus and common names are discussed in the note on Alpine Speedwell (*V. wormskjoldii*), shown on page 190. The species name, *filiformis*, refers to the thin filamentous stems of the flowers. These stems lead to another locally common name for the plant, Threadstalk Speedwell. Two other common allied plants occur in the area. Cusick's Speedwell (*V. cusickii*), is an erect species up to 20 cm tall that occurs in higher elevations and has blue flowers in terminal clusters, with stamens and styles protruding from the corolla. American Brookline (*V. americana*) grows up to 80 cm tall in wet ground and shallow water at middle elevations. It has few blue flowers with a yellow throat.

Small-Flowered Blue-Eyed Mary
Collinsia parviflora

FIGWORT FAMILY

This small, early-blooming annual grows on open slopes, mossy outcrops, and grassy areas from the lower to middle elevations. The plant has single or branched stems that are slender and weak, causing the plant to sprawl. The leaves are opposite, narrowly egg-shaped to linear, and tapered to the base and tip. The upper leaves often appear in whorls of three to five leaflets. The small flowers are two-lipped, pale blue and white on the upper lip and blue on the lower lip, and emerge from the axils of the upper leaves. The petals are fused at the base and the corolla tube is abruptly bent at an oblique angle near the base. The upper lip has two lobes and the lower has three, with the middle lobe being folded inward.

The genus name, *Collinsia*, honours Zaccheus Collins, a 19-century American botanist and mineralogist who was vice president of the Philadelphia Academy of Natural Sciences. The species name, *parviflora*, is derived from the Greek *parvus*, which means "small," and *flora*, which means "flower." Thomas Nuttall named the genus and David Douglas named the species in 1827. Douglas shipped seeds for the plant to England, where it was grown and scientifically described.

The reference to Mary in the common name is said to be to the mother of Jesus, but how that reference came about is a mystery. The plant also goes by the locally common names Small Pimpernel, Blue Lips, and Maiden Blue-Eyed Mary. A similar species, Large-Flowered Blue-Eyed Mary (*C. grandiflora*), occurs in similar habitat, but, as its name would suggest, it has larger flowers.

Small-Flowered Penstemon (Slender Beardtongue)
Penstemon procerus

FIGWORT FAMILY

This plant grows 40 cm tall at low to alpine elevations, usually in dry to moist open forests, grassy clearings, meadows, and disturbed areas. Most of the blunt to lance-shaped leaves appear in opposite pairs up the stem. The flowers are small, funnel-shaped, blue to purple, and appear in one to several tight clusters arranged in whorls around the stem and at its tip.

The common name, Beardtongue, describes the hairy, tongue-like staminode (sterile stamen) in the throat of the flower. The genus name, *Penstemon*, originates from the Greek *pente*, meaning "five," and *stemon*, meaning "stamen," five being the total number of stamens in the flower. The genus is a large and complex group of plants. There are many different Penstemons in the region, and often they will hybridize freely, adding even more confusion to the specific identification. This plant can usually be identified by its small, tightly packed blue flowers that appear in whorls around the stem, often in interrupted clusters. The species name, *procerus*, is derived from Latin and means "very tall," which is somewhat peculiar because this plant is not usually very tall. Other common names applied to the plant are Slender Beardtongue, Slender Blue Beardtongue, and Small-Flowered Beardtongue.

King Gentian
Gentiana sceptrum

GENTIAN FAMILY

Virginia Skilton image

This beautiful plant occurs in bogs, wet meadows, and lake margins at low elevations. The plant may have one or more flowering stems up to 1 m tall. The leaves are oblong-lanceolate and occur in 10 to 15 opposite pairs distributed up the stem, with the largest leaves near the top of the stem. The lowest leaves are reduced to short bracts. The tubular flowers are blue, often spotted or streaked with green, five-lobed, with pleats between the lobes. The flowers usually occur in a cluster atop the stem, with others on short stalks in the axils of the upper leaves.

The origin of the genus name, *Gentiana*, is explained in the note on Northern Gentian (*G. amarella*), shown on page 197. The species name, *sceptrum*, arises because the blue flowers atop the stem are said to be reminiscent of a sceptre, the staff carried by a king or queen as a symbol of sovereignty. Hence the common names King Gentian and King's Scepted Gentian. Flowers in this genus have folds or accordion-like pleats between the petal lobes. Flowers in the related genus *Gentianella* do not have pleats between the petal lobes, and display a fringe in the throat of the flower.

Northern Gentian
Gentianella amarella (also *Gentiana amarella*)

GENTIAN FAMILY

A plant of moist places in meadows, woods, ditches, and stream banks, up to the subalpine zone. These lovely flowers are first sighted by their star-like formation winking at the top of the corolla tube, amidst adjacent grasses. The plant is most often small, standing only 15–20 cm, though taller specimens are sometimes seen. The flowers appear in clusters in the axils of the upper stem leaves, the leaves being opposite and appearing almost to be small hands holding up the flowers for inspection. There is a fringe inside the throat of the flower.

The genus name, *Gentianella*, comes from Gentius, a king of ancient Illyria, a coastal region on the Adriatic Sea. Gentius was said to have discovered medicinal properties in the plants of this genus. Gentians have been used as medicinal tonics for centuries. The species name, *amarella*, is derived from the Latin *amarus*, meaning "bitter," a reference to the bitter alkaloids contained in the plant's juices. The plant is also commonly referred to as Autumn Dwarf Gentian and Felwort. The latter name is derived from Old English *feld*, which means "field," and *wort*, which means "herb" or "a plant." Flowers in the genus *Gentianella* do not have pleats between the petal lobes. Flowers in the related genus *Gentiana* do have a pleat between the petal lobes and lack the fringe in the throat of the flower.

Harebell
Campanula rotundifolia

HAREBELL FAMILY

This plant is widespread in a variety of habitats, including grasslands, gullies, moist forests, openings, clearings and rocky open ground. The flowers are purplish-blue, rarely white, bell-shaped, with hairless sepals, nodding on a thin stem in loose clusters. The leaves are thin on the stem and lance-shaped. The basal leaves are heart-shaped and coarsely toothed, but they usually wither before the flowers appear.

The genus name, *Campanula*, is derived from the Latin *campana*, meaning "bell." *Campanula* is the diminutive of *campana*, thus "little bell." The species name, *rotundifolia*, refers to the round basal leaves. This is the Bluebell of Scotland, and one school of thought holds that Harebell comes from a contraction of "heatherbell." Another school of thought holds that Harebell is a misspelling of "hairbell," the reference being to the hair-thin stems on which the flowers appear. Where Harebells occur, they can be in profusion and can cast a purple hue to the area when they are in bloom. The Cree were said to have chopped and dried the roots to make into compresses to stop bleeding and reduce swelling. The foliage contains alkaloids and is avoided by browsing animals.

Hairy Honeysuckle
Lonicera hispidula

HONEYSUCKLE FAMILY

This is a woody, climbing vine or spreading shrub that clambers over trees and other vegetation in woodlands and forest openings at low to middle elevations. The leaves are broadly elliptic, stiffly hairy, up to 10 cm long, and opposite on the stem, except the uppermost pairs, which are connate, that is, fused at their bases to form a shallow cup through which the stem passes. The flowers are purple to pink, tubular, up to 2 cm long, and appear in clusters of 5 to 25 blooms from inside the connate leaves. The fruits are bright red berries which are edible but very tart.

The origin of the genus name, *Lonicera*, is discussed in the note on Black Twinberry (*L. involucrata*), shown on page 256. The species name, *hispidula*, refers to the hairs on the plant. Orange Honeysuckle (*L. ciliosa*), shown on page 41, is a related species that appears in similar habitat. It has a cluster of large orange flowers in its connate leaves. Native peoples used the stems of honeysuckles to fashion woven mats, bags, baskets, and blankets.

Narrow-Leaved Blue-Eyed Grass
Sisyrinchium angustifolium

IRIS FAMILY

These beautiful flowers can be found scattered among the grasses of moist meadows from low to the subalpine elevations. The distinctively flattened stems grow to 30 cm tall, and are twice as tall as the grass-like basal leaves. The blue flower is star-shaped, with three virtually identical petals and sepals, each tipped with a minute point. There is a bright yellow eye in the centre of the flower. The blossoms are very short-lived, wilting usually within one day, to be replaced by fresh ones the next day.

The genus name, *Sisyrinchium*, was a name applied by Theophrastus, a disciple of Aristotle who refined the philosopher's work in botany and natural sciences in ancient Greece. It is a reference to a plant allied to the Iris. The species name, *angustifolium*, is Latin meaning "narrow-leaved." The flower has a number of locally common names, including Blue-Eyed Grass, Eyebright, Grass Widow, and Blue Star.

Satin Flower
Olsynium douglasii (formerly *Sisyrinchium douglasii*)

IRIS FAMILY

These beautiful flowers bloom very early in the spring in dry, open, rocky areas, and in meadows and open woods that are seasonally wet in the spring but dry later in the year. The somewhat flattened flower stems grow up to 30 cm tall, taller than the grass-like basal leaves. The flowers, solitary to several, are bell-like, up to 3 cm wide, with six deep reddish-purple tepals, rounded at the ends. Inside the bell hang three yellow-tipped stamens and an elongated style that is three-pronged.

Once classified in the genus *Sisyrinchium*, Satin Flower is now the only North American species in the allied genus *Olsynium*. The species name honours 19th-century Scottish explorer and botanist David Douglas, who first "discovered" the plant in 1826 near Celilo Falls in what is now the State of Oregon. Douglas, for whom the Douglas fir is also named, was one of the most prolific and travelled collectors of botanical specimens of his time. Many Native peoples referred to him as "Man Who Saves Grass!" The flower has a number of locally common names, including Grass Widow, Purple-Eyed Grass, Douglas' Blue-Eyed Grass, and Douglas' Grass Widow.

Chocolate Lily (Checker Lily)
Fritillaria affinis (formerly *F. lanceolata*)

LILY FAMILY

Virginia Skilton image

This early-blooming upright perennial grows up to 80 cm tall in variable habitat that includes prairies, grassy bluffs, woodlands, and conifer forests from sea level to the montane zone. The plant grows from a cluster of bulbs and small offsets that resemble grains of rice. Indeed, a locally common name for the plant is Rice Root. The narrow, lance-shaped leaves are up to 15 cm long, and all are borne on the stem, mostly arranged in one or two imperfect whorls of three to five leaves. Several nodding flowers occur in a loose raceme up the stem. Each individual flower has six purple tepals, checked with yellow, giving the flower a dark brown appearance, and giving rise to another common name, Chocolate Lily. The flowers are ill-scented, described variously as smelling of rotten meat or dirty socks. This foul odour is probably an allure to flies as pollinators. The fruit is an upright cylindrical capsule with six wings.

The genus name, *Fritillaria,* is derived from the Latin *fritillus,* which means "dice box," most probably a reference to the fruit, which appears as an erect, cylindrical capsule. The first specimen collected for science was gathered by Meriwether Lewis in April 1806 on the Columbia River in what is now the State of Oregon. Mission Bells is another locally common name applied to the plant. Northern Riceroot (*F. camschatcensis*), shown on page 205, is an allied plant that occurs in coastal areas. It has leaves in three main whorls of five to ten leaves, and has several bell-shaped, nodding flowers that appear in the axils of the upper leaves.

Early Camas
Camassia quamash

LILY FAMILY

This plant of wet meadows and stream banks has long, narrow grass-like leaves, and a tall, naked stem. The startling blue to purplish flowers (occasionally white) are numerous, and appear in a loose cluster at the top of the stem. The flowers have six tepals that are spreading and somewhat unevenly spaced. The stamens are golden, and contrast vividly with the blue inflorescence of the plant.

The genus and species names for this plant are derived from the names given to the plant by the Nimi'-pu, or Nez Perce people. In September 1805, Captain William Clark of the Lewis and Clark expedition, came upon some Nez Perce digging the bulbs of the plant for food. The Nez Perce shared the bulbs with the members of the expedition, at a time when food had grown scarce for the expedition. The onion-like bulbs were a very important food for Native peoples, trappers, and settlers in western North America. The bulbs were baked, boiled, roasted, eaten raw, and ground into flour for baking bread. So important were the bulbs, that local wars were fought over the rights to certain large meadows where the plants grew in profusion. Victoria, British Columbia, was once called Camosun, meaning "a place for gathering camas." Great Camas (*C. leichtlinii*) is a similar species that occurs in the same habitat. It generally is a taller plant, bearing more flowers of a greater colour range, and blooming later than Early Camas.

Harvest Brodiaea
Brodiaea coronaria

LILY FAMILY

This plant grows from a dark brown, scaly, globe-shaped corm in dry meadows and grasslands. The corm puts up an erect, stout, leafless, flowering stem that is up to 30 cm tall. There are one to three basal leaves that are linear and almost as tall as the flowering stem, but they wither prior to blooming. The flowers are funnel- to bell-shaped, violet to purple with darker midlines on the petal centres, and have three white sterile stamens inside the whitish floral cup. The flowers occur in a loose umbel of two to ten erect to spreading, unequally stalked flowers at the top of the stem.

The genus name, *Brodiaea*, honours 19th-century Scottish botanist James Brodie. The species name, *coronaria* means "used for or belonging to garlands or crowns." Indeed, another locally common name for the plant is Crown Brodiaea. Native peoples and early settlers dug the corms for food, eating them raw or cooked. They are said to be very nutritious and pleasantly flavoured.

Northern Riceroot (Kamchatka Lily)
Fritillaria camschatcensis

LILY FAMILY

Doug Skilton image

This upright perennial grows up to 60 cm tall from a scaly bulb with numerous rice-like bulblets, which give the plant some of its common names. It favours habitat that is continually moist, and is found from sea level to the subalpine. The leaves occur on the stem in whorls of five to ten lance-shaped leaves up to 6 cm long. The widely bell-shaped, nodding flowers are purple-brown to bronze to liver-coloured to almost black, and occur in the axils of the upper leaves. The petals are slightly reflexed and exhibit small parallel ridges on the inside. The fruits are erect, barrel-shaped, bluntly six-angled, and have no wings as seen in the related species, Chocolate Lily. The flowers are ill-scented, being variously described as smelling of rotten meat or dirty socks. This foul odour is probably an allure to flies as pollinators.

The origin of the genus name, *Fritillaria,* is discussed in the narrative on Chocolate Lily (*F. affinis*), shown on page 202. The species name, *camschatcensis,* is a reference to the Kamchatka Peninsula in northeastern Asia, apparently where the plant was first found and described for science. The plant goes by a number of locally common names, including Black Lily, Kamchatka Lily, Indian Rice, Rice Lily, Eskimo Potato, Skunk Lily, Dirty Diaper, and Outhouse Lily. The bulbs of the plant were used extensively as food by Native peoples, prepared in various ways.

Spanish Bluebell
Hyacinthoides hispanica

LILY FAMILY

This plant blooms in the spring in meadows and open woods, often forming extensive clumps of blue, pink, and/or white flowers. The basal leaves are few, linear or oblong, 20–50 cm long, and up to 3.5 cm across. The leaves are erect on emergence, but become floppy and tend to spread on the ground later in the blooming period. The inflorescence occurs as a loose spike of numerous flowers at the top of a bare stem. The flowers have six petals that are fused together at the base to form a wide, open bell. Each flower has two linear to lanceolate bracts at the base of the flower stalk.

The genus name, *Hyacinthoides*, is derived from the Greek *hyacinthine*, which means "light violet or purple-blue," and *oides*, which means "same as" or "similar to," a reference to the colour of the flowers resembling hyacinths. The specific name, *hispanica*, means "of Spain" or "Spanish." The plant was formerly known as *Scilla hispanica*, which gives rise to two locally common names, Scilla and Squill.

Heal-All (Self-Heal)
Prunella vulgaris

MINT FAMILY

This is a plant found in moist woods, along stream banks and lakeshores and in fields from the prairie to the montane zone. The flowers occur in terminal clusters, usually surrounded by the upper leaves. The bracts are kidney-shaped to oval, with spines at the tips and hairs along the margins. The few leaves are opposite, smooth and sparsely hairy. The plant is small and sprawling, and square-stemmed.

The genus name, *Prunella,* is most likely derived from the German *bräune,* meaning "quinsy," or angina tonsillaris, a condition this plant was used to cure. The traditional use of the plant for healing internal and external bleeding gives rise to the common names, but tests on the plant's extracts have not revealed any biochemical basis for the claims of healing. Parts of this small flower have been used by Native peoples to relieve boils, cuts, bruises, swelling and internal bleeding. The Cree treated sore throats with an extract from the plant. The Blackfoot used it as an eyewash and treated horses' saddle sores with it. The leaves can be brewed into a tea.

Wild Mint (Canada Mint)
Mentha arvensis (also *M. canadensis*)

MINT FAMILY

This plant inhabits wetland marshes, moist woods, banks and shores of streams and lakes, and sometimes lives in shallow water. The purplish, to pinkish, to bluish flowers are crowded in dense clusters in the upper leaf axils. The leaves are opposite, prominently veined, and highly scented of mint if crushed. The stems are square in cross-section and hairy.

The genus name, *Mentha*, is from the Greek *Minthe*, a mythological nymph loved by Pluto. A jealous Proserpine changed the nymph into a mint plant. The species name, *arvensis*, means "of cultivated fields." The strong, distinctive taste of mint plants is from their volatile oils. The leaves have long been used fresh, dried, and frozen as a flavouring and for teas. Some Native peoples used the leaves to flavour meat and pemmican, and lined dried-meat containers with mint leaves prior to winter storage. Strong mint teas were used by Native peoples and European settlers as a treatment for coughs, colds, and fevers. Wild Mint often occurs in extensive patches.

Dame's Rocket (Dame's Violet)
Hesperis matronalis

MUSTARD FAMILY

This member of the mustard family was introduced from Eurasia into North America during colonial days as an ornamental plant, and it has spread extensively, now being found throughout Canada and much of the United States. In many areas it is looked upon as an invasive, noxious weed, though it is still available and sold as an ornamental by some nurseries. Typically it inhabits disturbed sites, waste ground, thickets, woods, and road and railsides. The plant is erect and grows to over 1 m tall. The leaves are alternate, lance-shaped, predominantly clasping on the stem, hairy on both sides, and become progressively smaller up the stem. The flowers occur in showy clusters at the top of the stem. Each flower is four-petalled, purple to blue to white, and fragrant.

The genus name, *Hesperis*, is derived from the Greek *hesperos*, which means "evening," the reference being that the flowers are said to have an enhanced aroma near evening. The species name, *matronalis*, is said to derive from the flower being a favourite of Roman matrons, ergo the reference to Dame in the common name. Dame's Rocket goes by a number of other common names, including Dame's Violet, Dames Wort, Sweet Rocket, and Mother of the Evening.

Bittersweet (Purple Nightshade)
Solanum dulcamara

NIGHTSHADE FAMILY

This plant is a Eurasian import that has become a noxious weed in many parts of North America, occurring most often in damp to wet thickets, clearings, and open woods. It is a low, climbing, scrambling, sprawling vine that drapes itself over low trees and shrubs. The leaves are alternate, simple, entire, and broadly ovate with basal lobes. The flowers hang in loose clusters of 3 to 20 blooms. Each individual flower is up to 1.5 cm across, star-shaped with five purple petals that are reflexed backward, and yellow stamens and style pointing forward. The fruits are bright, shiny berries that resemble small tomatoes, hanging in clusters. The fruits start as green berries, then turn yellow, then orange, and finally red. Not all the berries turn colour at the same time, so the plant can display berries of various colours.

The genus name, *Solanum*, is derived from Latin and means "quietening" or "soothing," a reference to the narcotic properties of some members of the genus. The species name, *dulcamara*, literally means "sweetbitter," which reverses to be one of the common names applied to the plant. All parts of this plant are extremely poisonous to humans and livestock. Though poisonous, the plant has found usage in homeopathic and herbal medicine, and is considered to be an important remedy for treating herpes infections and allergies. This plant is not related in any way to Enchanter's Nightshade (*Circaea alpina*), shown on page 94.

Alfalfa
Medicago sativa

PEA FAMILY

Alfalfa is an introduced species that was brought to North America as a forage crop for livestock. It has escaped from cultivated fields and is now locally common in roadside ditches and rights-of-way. The leaves are elliptic to oblong, and occur in threes. They are slightly hairy, and sharply toothed at the tips. The flowers are pea-like, purple to blue, and occur in oblong-shaped clusters. The fruits are spirally coiled pods.

Alfalfa is said to have been cultivated as far back in history as the Medes in ancient Persia. The Greeks introduced the plant to Europe at the time of the Persian wars. Black Medick (*M. lupulina*) is a close relative of Alfalfa found in the same habitat. Black Medick has yellow flowers, and its fruit is less tightly coiled than Alfalfa's and turns black at maturity. Alfalfa is similar to another common introduced species, Sweet-Clover (*Melilotus* spp.), but Alfalfa generally has narrower and more wedge-shaped leaves that are toothed only near the tip.

Bicoloured Lupine (Miniature Lupine)
Lupinus bicolor

PEA FAMILY

This small, annual Lupine stands more or less erect with flowering stems that grow up to 40 cm tall in coastal and low, moist areas. The leaves appear only on the stem, and they are alternate, palmately compound, with five to eight leaflets that are linear, sharp-pointed to blunt on the tip, and hairy on both sides. The flowers occur in a raceme at the top of the flowering stem. The wings and keel on the flowers are blue, the oblong to circular banner is blue with a white stripe down its centre, and the keel is fringed with hair.

The genus name, *Lupinus*, is derived from *lupus*, the "wolf." It is said that this name is a reference to the once held belief that Lupines devoured or robbed soil nutrients where they grew. In fact, Lupines have nitrogen-fixing bacteria in their root nodules, and they actually improve poor soil. Two other similarly coloured small Lupines occur in the area. Small-Flowered Lupine (*L. polycarpus*) has a banner that is heart-shaped. Low Mountain Lupine (*L. lyallii*) is a silvery hairy mat-like plant of the alpine meadows with short flowering stems.

Large-leaved Lupine (Bigleaf Lupine)
Lupinus polyphyllus

PEA FAMILY

This plant has erect stems that stand up to 1.5 m tall in fields, at roadsides, and in moist ground, from low to montane elevations. The stems are usually unbranched, cylindrical, and hollow at the base. The few basal leaves are on long stalks, while the stem leaves are alternate and on shorter stalks. The leaves are palmately compound, with 9 to 17 leaflets that are elliptic, pointed at the tip, smooth on top and sparsely hairy below. The inflorescence occurs at the top of the stem in a dense raceme of stalked, whorled and scattered, bluish to violet pea-like flowers. The plant is quite handsome and impressive. It often forms large colonies.

The origin of the genus name is discussed in the note on Bicoloured Lupine (*L. bicolor*), shown on page 212. The specific name means "many leaves." There are a number of Lupines in the region and all have very characteristic leaves and flowers. Arctic Lupine (*L. arcticus*) occurs in alpine meadows, stands up to 75 cm tall, and has purplish-blue flowers with white accents on the outer edges of the banner and the top of the keel.

Tufted Vetch (Bird Vetch)
Vicia cracca

PEA FAMILY

This plant thrives in shady riverine habitats, open woods, thickets, and meadows. The purple flowers are typical of the pea family. The leaves are alternate, pinnately divided, and have forked tendrils at the ends of the leaves. The plant creeps and climbs over adjacent plants.

The genus name, *Vicia*, is derived from the Latin *vincire*, which means "to bind together," referring to the binding tendrils on the leaves. *Vicia* was apparently translated to Old North French as *veche*, and later became the English word *vetch*. The species name, *cracca*, is the Latin name for Vetch. Vetches can build nitrates in soil and are looked upon as good forage for livestock. Vetches are sometimes difficult to differentiate from peas (genus *Lathyrus*). The flower in question must be examined closely, perhaps even under low magnification. Pinch the keel to expose the pistil. In Vetches the style has hairs arranged all around, like a bottle brush; in peas the style has hairs only on one side, like a toothbrush.

Jacob's Ladder (Showy Jacob's Ladder)
Polemonium pulcherrimum

PHLOX FAMILY

This beautiful plant grows in dry, open, rocky environments in the montane to alpine zones. The leaves are distinctive. They are pinnately compound, with 11 to 25 round to elliptic leaflets that are evenly spaced to resemble a tiny ladder. The leaf arrangement gives the plant its common name – a reference to the story in the Bible book of Genesis wherein Jacob found a ladder to heaven. The pale to dark blue, cup-shaped flowers appear in an open cluster at the top of the stem. The flowers have a vivid orange ring at the base of the cup. The plant is covered with glandular hairs, which are said to impart the foul odour of the plant.

There are two schools of thought as to the origin of the genus name, *Polemonium.* One school holds that the name comes from the Greek philosopher Polemon. The other holds that the name is derived from the Greek word *polemos*, which means "strife." According to this school of thought, a dispute as to who discovered the plant, and its supposed medicinal properties, sparked a war between two kings! The species name is derived from the Latin *pulcher*, which means "beautiful" or "very handsome." The plant is apparently a favourite of bees.

Moss Campion
Silene acaulis

PINK FAMILY

This low-growing, ground-hugging cushion plant occupies in an alpine environment in rock crevices and on cliffs and exposed ridges. The bright green, narrow leaves are linear to narrowly lance-shaped, arise from the base of the plant, and often form cushions up to 1 m in diameter, resembling moss. Dead leaves from previous seasons often persist for years. The small, pink, five-lobed, tubular flowers are borne on single, short stalks, but they often appear to be sitting on the mossy surface.

There is some contention about the origin of the genus name, *Silene*. Some authorities assert that the name originates from the Greek *sialon*, which means "saliva," a reference to the gummy exudation on the stems of some members of the genus. Others contend that the name is derived from Silenus, the besotted father of Bacchus (the god of wine), who was covered with foam, again a reference to the glandular secretions of some members of the genus. The species name, *acaulis*, means "not stalked," a reference to the stalkless appearance of the flowers. While this is an alpine species, it is often grown in rock gardens, and is easily propagated from seeds.

Broad-Leaved Shooting Star
Dodecatheon hendersonii

PRIMROSE FAMILY

This beautiful plant is scattered and locally common at low elevations in warm, dry grassy meadows and open woods. The basal leaves appear in a rosette and are egg-shaped, narrowing abruptly to the stalk. The numerous flowers appear nodding atop a leafless stalk. The flowers are purple to lavender with corolla lobes turned backward. The stamens are united into a dark purplish or black tube, from which the style and anthers protrude.

A harbinger of spring, these lovely flowers can bloom in huge numbers. The genus name, *Dodecatheon*, is derived from the Greek *dodeka*, meaning "twelve," and *theos*, meaning "gods," thus a plant that is protected by twelve gods. The species name, *hendersonii*, honours 20th–century American botanist Louis Fourniquet Henderson, who lived and worked in the Pacific Northwest. Native peoples used an infusion from this plant as an eyewash, and some looked upon the plant as a charm to obtain wealth. Some tribes mashed the flowers to make a pink dye for their arrows. The common name is an apt description of the flower, with the turned-back petals streaming behind the stamens. Few-Flowered Shooting Star (*D. pulchellum*) is a similar species that appears in the region. It has more lance-shaped leaves, the stamen tube is yellowish to orange, and it usually have fewer flowers.

Marsh Cinquefoil
Potentilla palustris

ROSE FAMILY

This plant inhabits bogs, marshes, streams, and ponds from the valleys to the subalpine zone. It grows from long, smooth rhizomes, creeping along the ground and rooting at the nodes. The leaves are usually smooth and pinnately compound, with five to seven obovate (teardrop-shaped) leaflets that are deeply toothed. While other members of the *Potentilla* family have yellow or white/cream coloured flowers, Marsh Cinquefoil has purple to deep red flowers.

The origin of the genus name, *Potentilla*, is explained in the note on Silverweed (*P. anserina*), shown on page 266. The species name, *palustris*, is derived from the Latin *palus*, which means "marsh" or "swamp," a reference to the favoured habitat of the plant. The flowers have an offensive, rotten odour that attracts insects as pollinators. The plant is also known by the locally common name Purple Marshlocks.

Purple Saxifrage (Purple Mountain Saxifrage)
Saxifraga oppositifolia

SAXIFRAGE FAMILY

Tracy Utting image

This plant is a very low, matted, cushion-forming plant, with tightly packed stems, common to the rocky talus slopes, ledges, and boulder fields in the alpine zone, particularly on calcium-rich substrates. The five-petalled purple to pink flowers appear singly on short stems. The leaves are opposite, stalkless, and appear whorled. Each leaf is broadly wedge-shaped, and bluish-green.

The genus name, *Saxifraga*, is derived from the Latin *saxum*, meaning "rock," and *frangere*, meaning "to break," a reference to the belief that plants in the genus are capable of breaking rocks into soil. The species name, *oppositifolia*, refers to the opposite arrangement of the leaves. The plant blooms early in the year, and given its blooming time and its somewhat inaccessible habitat, it is often gone before it is seen by many people. Purple Saxifrage is the official flower of the Territory of Nunavut.

Western Long-Spurred Violet (Early Blue Violet)
Viola adunca

VIOLET FAMILY

A plant of the grasslands, open woods, and slopes, this violet is widespread in North America and is highly variable. The flower colour ranges from blue to purple, and the three lower petals are often whitish at the base, pencilled with darker purple guidelines. The largest petal has a hooked spur half as long as the lower petal. The leaves are mostly basal, oval with a heart-shaped base, and have round teeth on the margins. The plant grows low to the ground.

The genus name, *Viola*, is derived from the Latin *violaceous*, for the purple colour. The species name, *adunca*, means "hooked," a reference to the hook on the spur of the flower. An *uncus* was a hook used by the Romans to drag executed bodies away from the place of execution. Violets have been used for food for centuries. The leaves are high in vitamins A and C, and can be used to make a bland tea. Violet seeds have special oily bodies called elaiosomes, which attract ants. The ants carry the seeds away to their nests, thus dispersing the seeds. Common garden Pansies are also a member of the *Viola* family.

Silky Phacelia (Silky Scorpionweed)
Phacelia sericea

WATERLEAF FAMILY

This spectacular plant grows on dry, rocky, open slopes at moderate to high elevations. The leaves are deeply divided into many segments and covered with silky hairs. The purple to blue flowers occur in clusters up a spike, resembling a bottle brush. The individual flowers are funnel-shaped, with long, purple, yellow-tipped stamens sticking out. The clusters of coiled branches resemble scorpion tails, thus the common name.

The genus name, *Phacelia*, is derived from the Greek *phakelos*, meaning "bundle," a reference to the dense flower clusters. The species name, *sericea*, means "silky," a reference to the fine hairs on the plant. Some people experience a dermatological reaction if they handle the plant. The flowers of this plant are quite stunning, and having once seen it, one is unlikely to forget it.

Thread-leaved Phacelia (Thread-leaved Scorpionweed)
Phacelia linearis

WATERLEAF FAMILY

This annual species of *Phacelia* occurs in the southern part of the area, but is more common east of the coastal mountains. It grows to 50 cm tall, and appears on dry plateaus and foothills. The leaves are hairy, alternate, thin and linear below, developing side lobes higher on the stem. The flowers are reasonably large, lavender to blue and appearing in open clusters from the leaf axils.

The origin of the genus name, *Phacelia*, is discussed in the note on Silky Phacelia (*P. sericea*), shown on page 221. The common name, Scorpionweed, arises because some people say the coiled branches of the flower clusters resemble the tail of a scorpion. The first specimen of the species was collected by Meriwether Lewis in the spring of 1806 near present-day The Dalles, Oregon.

Yellow Flowers

This section includes flowers that are
predominantly yellow when encountered in
the field. The colour varies from bright yellow to
pale cream. Some of the flowers in this section have
other colour variations and you may have to
check other sections of the book to find the flower.
For example, the Paintbrushes (*Castilleja* sp) have a
yellow variation, but they are most often encountered
in a red colour and they have been pictured in
that section for purposes of sorting.

Skunk Cabbage (Yellow Arum)
Lysichiton americanum

ARUM FAMILY

This early-blooming distinctive perennial grows in large patches from a fleshy rhizome, and inhabits swamps, bogs, marshes, and mucky ground at low to middle elevations. The inflorescence appears before the leaves. The inflorescence consists of hundreds of tiny, greenish-yellow flowers sunk into a thick, fleshy stalk known as a spadix, which is surrounded by a large, bright yellow sheath leaf known as a spathe. The broadly elliptic leaves are huge, growing up to 120 cm long on stout stalks. Though it does not actually smell of skunk, the whole plant has an earthy odour, giving rise to the common name. The scent attracts beetles as pollinators.

The genus name, *Lysichiton*, is derived from the Greek *lysis*, which means "loosening," and *chiton*, which means "tunic," a reference to the spathe unfolding from around the spadix. The plant contains needle-like crystals of calcium oxalate which will pierce the lining in the mouth, but those crystals are eliminated when the roots are dried or roasted. Native peoples dried and roasted the plant, then ground it into a flour. The large leaves were used as liners in food-steaming pits and baskets, and as a wrapping material for other foods. The plant is also locally called Swamp Lantern, a reference to the large yellow spathe standing out amidst the dark green background of its preferred habitat. Bears also eat the whole plant, and deer browse on the leaves. The plant is related to taro.

Oregon Grape
Mahonia nervosa (formerly *Berberis nervosa*)

BARBERRY FAMILY

This evergreen shrub is widespread and common at low to middle elevations in dry plateaus and dry to moist forests and openings in the foothills. The plant very closely resembles holly, with shiny, sharp-pointed leaves that turn to lovely orange and rusty colours in the fall. The flowers are pale to bright yellow, round, and bloom in the early spring, giving way to a small purple berry that resembles a grape.

The genus name, *Mahonia*, honours 18th-century Irish-born horticulturist Bernard M'Mahon, who moved to Pennsylvania in 1796 to start a nursery. The specific name, *nervosa*, means "having distinct veins or nerves," a reference to the leaves of the plant. Plants in the genus were once classified in genus *Berberis*, which was the Latinized form of the Arabic name for the barberry fruit. The fruits are very bitter tasting from the plant, but make a delicious jelly when processed. Native peoples extracted a bright yellow pigment from the inner bark and roots of the plant, and used it to dye basket material. The inner bark was also used for medicinal purposes, including easing child delivery, healing wounds, combating infections, and treating venereal disease. Tall Oregon Grape (*M. aquifolium*) is a similar plant in the region, but it grows to much larger sizes than does this species. Its flowers, fruits, and leaves are virtually identical to those of this species.

Common Bladderwort
Utricularia vulgaris

BLADDERWORT FAMILY

This aquatic carnivorous plant is found in shallow water in sloughs, lakes, ditches, and ponds. It floats beneath the surface of the water, with a tangle of coarse stems and leaves. The long, branching, submerged stems have finely divided leaves that spread out like small nets. Attached to the leaves hang numerous small bladders that are actually traps for aquatic insects. When an insect swims into the bladders, small hairs are tripped, which shuts the bladder, trapping the insect inside. The insects are then digested, providing a source of nitrogen for the plant. The yellow flowers appear on leafless stalks that extend above the surface of the water. The corolla of the flower is two-lipped, with brown stripes on the throat. The floral tube extends into a short, spur-like sac at the base.

The genus name, *Utricularia*, is derived from the Latin *utriculus*, which means "small bottle" or "little bag," a reference to the bladders on the plants. The species name, *vulgaris*, means "common."

Poque (Ground-cone)
Boschniakia hookeri

BROOMRAPE FAMILY

Doug Skilton images

This intriguing plant is parasitic and grows on rocky coastal bluffs and open slopes from a coarse, fleshy root that puts up a single, stout stem up to 3 cm thick and 15 cm tall. There are no leaves, just scaly bracts that are alternate and overlapping, giving the plant the appearance of a large conifer cone sitting upright on the ground. The inflorescence is numerous small flowers in the spike, each one subtended by a bract. The flowers are yellow to purple, and have two lips, with the lower lip shorter than the upper. The plant often forms clumps, and it is most often parasitic on Salal (*Gaulthera shallon*), shown on page 39, and Hairy Manzanita (*Arctostaphylos columbiana*), shown on page 100. The colour of the plant can vary, but the conifer cone shape is distinctive and unmistakable.

The genus name, *Boschniakia*, honours 19th-century Russian botanist Alexander Karlovich Boschniak. The species name, *hookeri*, commemorates English botanist William Jackson Hooker, director of Kew Gardens in England, also in the 19th-century. Poque is the name attributed to the plant by Native peoples, who used it as food. The alternative names include Ground-Cone and Vancouver Ground-Cone.

Creeping Buttercup
Ranunculus repens

BUTTERCUP FAMILY

This European invader spreads over the ground by slender, creeping stems or runners, similar to those of the Wild Strawberry. The leaf blades are long-stalked, egg- or heart-shaped, and have scalloped margins. The plant is found in moist meadows, on stream banks, and at the margins of lakes and ponds.

Buttercups are among the oldest of flower families, having existed for millions of years before earliest man developed, and are considered one of the most primitive plant families. The cell structure on the petals is such that there is air in the cell vacuoles, and this is responsible for the "whiteness" seen on the petals. The genus name, *Ranunculus*, is from the Greek *rana*, which means "frog," a likely reference to the wetland or marshy habitat of many species in the family. The species name, *repens*, is Latin for "creeping," exactly descriptive of this plant. It has now extended its range from coast to coast and even into Alaska and the Yukon Territory.

Mountain Buttercup
Ranunculus eschscholtzii

BUTTERCUP FAMILY

This Buttercup can reach heights of 30 cm, and lives near or above timberline, appearing beside streams or ponds, near snowdrifts, and around late snowmelt. The leaves are mainly basal, sometimes deeply lobed, and round to kidney-shaped. The flowering stems are hairless and may accommodate up to three flowers. The flowers are bright yellow, with five petals and five purple-tinged sepals. Stamens and pistils are numerous.

The origin of the genus name, *Ranunculus*, is discussed in the note on Creeping Buttercup (*R. repens*), shown on page 228. The species name, *eschscholtzii*, honours Johann Friedrich Gustav von Eschscholtz, a 19th-century Estonian surgeon and professor of anatomy who accompanied two Russian explorations of the Pacific coast of North America. The California Poppy (*Eschscholzia californica*), shown on page 262, is also named for him. Mountain Buttercup is also known locally as Alpine Buttercup, Snow Buttercup, and Snowpack Buttercup.

Footsteps of Spring (Snakeroot Sanicle)
Sanicula arctopoides

CARROT FAMILY

This perennial grows on coastal bluffs from a taproot, and has branching stems that are prostrate to ascending, up to 30 cm long. The basal leaves form a rosette on the ground, and are succulent, light in colour, triangular in shape, deeply palmately three-cleft, and up to 6 cm long and half again as wide. The stem leaves are smaller, irregularly toothed or lobed, and sessile. The inflorescence is several to many compact dome-shaped umbels of tiny yellow flowers, each surrounded by a ring of long bracts which resemble the spokes on a wheel.

The genus name, *Sanicula*, is derived from the Latin *sanare*, which means "to heal," a reference to a belief that infusions from certain Old World relatives of the plant had healing properties. Indeed, decoctions from several allied plants that grow in the North American prairies were used by Native peoples as a cure for snakebite, a practice that gives plants of this genus a common name of Snakeroot. The specific name, *arctopoides*, means "like genus *Arctopus*," an Old World member of the Carrot Family.

Pacific Sanicle (Western Snakeroot)
Sanicula crassicaulis

CARROT FAMILY

This single-stemmed perennial grows from a taproot in open woods at lower elevations, and on shaded wooded slopes up to middle elevations. The stem is erect and stands up to 120 cm tall. The basal and lower stem leaves are stalked, alternate, and palmately divided into three to five lobes. The upper stem leaves are few, more sessile, and smaller. The flowers are tiny and yellow, appearing in tight, 1 cm wide, rounded clusters at the top of the stem.

The origins of the common and genus names are discussed in the note on Footsteps of Spring (*S. arctopoides*), shown on page 230. The specific name, *crassicaulis*, means "thick-stemmed." Sierra Sanicle (*S. graveolens*) is a similar plant that appears in open forests and rocky slopes from low to middle elevations in the region. It has very similar flowers, shorter flowering stems, and usually has a shock of small palmately divided leaves immediately below the inflorescence.

Spring Gold (Bladder Parsnip)
Lomatium utriculatum

CARROT FAMILY

This plant grows on dry, open rocky slopes and bluffs, and in meadows at low elevations. It is a leafy, upright perennial that blooms early and lasts a long time. The leaves are mostly basal, pinnately compound, and much dissected into small narrow segments, resembling those of garden carrots. The yellow flowers are tiny and appear in several compound umbels at the top of the stems. The fruits are smooth, elliptic, single-seeded pods with wide lateral wings.

The origin of the genus name, *Lomatium*, is discussed in the note on Chocolate Tips (*L. dissectum*), shown on page 79. The species name, *utriculatum*, means "with a small, bladder-like, one-seeded fruit," another reference to the fruits. This plant was used as food by Native peoples, eating the roots raw, cooked or dried, and the young leaves and shoots as greens. They also made decoctions from the plant for medicinal purposes, using them for cleaning wounds or as a remedy for headaches and stomach disorders.

Canada Goldenrod
Solidago canadensis

COMPOSITE FAMILY

This is an upright perennial that grows from a creeping rhizome and often forms large colonies in moist soil in meadows, along stream banks, and on lakeshores. The flowering stem is solitary, up to 1 m tall or more, has many branches near the top, and is covered with short, dense hairs. The leaves are all on the stem, of relatively uniform size, and they are lance-shaped to linear, alternate, simple, sharply saw-toothed, and hairy. The flowers are tiny and yellow, occurring in dense, pyramid-shaped clusters at the tops of the stem branches. The branches may curve outward or downward. Each flower has yellow ray and disk florets.

The genus name, *Solidago*, is probably derived from the Latin *solido*, meaning "to make whole or heal," a reference to the supposed healing properties of plants in the genus. The species name indicates the widespread occurrence of the plant in Canada. *Solidago* is a complex and highly variable genus, and a number of the members of the genus bloom in the area. Specific identification can be difficult, and dissection and magnification might be required for absolutely accurate results. That degree of specificity is outside the ambit of this book. Some Native peoples ground the flowers of Golden-rods into a lotion and applied it to bee stings. The once claimed medicinal virtues of the plants are not supported by research results. Goldenrods are also often blamed for causing hay-fever in some people, but the pollen in the plants is too heavy to be borne by the wind.

Dandelion
Taraxacum officinale

COMPOSITE FAMILY

This common, introduced plant is found in a variety of habitats the world over, and it is probably the most recognizable flower in our area for most people. The bright yellow flowers have ray florets only, and appear at the top of a smooth stem that arises from a whorl of basal leaves that are lance- to spoon-shaped and deeply incised. The flowers appear from early in the spring until late in the fall, giving this plant undoubtedly the longest blooming time of any flower in our area.

Though everybody seems to recognize this flower, it is interesting to note that more than 1,000 kinds of Dandelions have been described, and specific identification can be difficult. The common name for this plant is thought to be a corruption of the French *dent de lion*, meaning "lion's tooth," a reference to the shape of the leaf. All parts of the plant are edible – the young leaves are eaten raw or cooked as greens, the roots are dried and ground as a coffee substitute, and the flowers can be used to make wine. Some people roll the flower heads in flour and deep-fry them, claiming they have a flavour similar to morel mushrooms when so prepared. The sap from the plant was used in Ireland to treat warts.

Gold Star (Common Spring Gold)
Crocidium multicaule

COMPOSITE FAMILY

Dave Ingram image

This plant is a delicate, multi-stemmed annual that grows from fibrous roots in dry, open places at lower elevations. The stems are erect to ascending, grow up to 30 cm tall, and are smooth except for woolly white hairs in the leaf axils. The basal leaves are stalked, spoon-shaped, and coarsely toothed and form tufts on the ground. The stem leaves are few and small, appearing more like linear bracts. The flowers are solitary at the top of the stems, have 5–12 yellow ray florets surrounding yellow disk florets, with the disk about 1 cm wide. The flower heads are subtended by thin bracts in a conical shape.

The genus name, *Crocidium*, is derived from the Greek *krokidion*, which is the diminutive for *krokys* or *krokydos* and means "a flock or nap on woolen cloth," a reference to the white hairs in the leaf axils. The species name, *multicaule*, means "many stems." This plant also goes by the locally common name Common Spring Gold. Another plant in the region goes by the common name Spring Gold (*Lomatium utriculatum*), shown on page 232, but it is an unrelated plant that is a member of the Carrot Family.

Gumweed (Puget Sound Gumweed)
Grindelia integrifolia

COMPOSITE FAMILY

This is a perennial herb that grows from a taproot, with several erect to ascending stems that are usually branched and up to 80 cm tall. The plant occurs at the edges of salt marshes, along rocky shores and in open meadows at low elevations. The basal leaves are alternate, oblong to lance-shaped, and up to 40 cm long and 4 cm wide. The stem leaves are smaller, unstalked, somewhat clasping, and are covered with long, soft hairs. The inflorescence is solitary composite heads 3 cm wide at the tops of the stems, each consisting of 10 to 35 yellow ray flowers surrounding yellow disk flowers. The flower heads are subtended by slender, green-tipped, sticky bracts that are loose or spreading, some being irregularly reflexed.

The genus name, *Grindelia*, honours David Hieronymus Grindel, a 19th-century Latvian chemist, pharmacologist, physician, and professor of botany at Riga. The species name, *integrifolia*, means that the leaf margins are entire – i.e., uncut or not toothed. The common name alludes to the sticky resins produced by the bracts. Native peoples used the plant medicinally to treat a variety of ailments.

Heart-leaved Arnica
Arnica cordifolia

COMPOSITE FAMILY

Arnica is a common plant of wooded areas in the mountains, foothills and boreal forest. The leaves occur in two to four opposite pairs along the stem, each with long stalks and heart-shaped, serrated blades. The uppermost pair is stalkless and more lance-shaped than the lower leaves. The flowers have 10 to 15 bright yellow ray florets and bright yellow central disk florets.

Without careful dissection of the plant and examination under magnification, recognition of specific members of the genus *Arnica* can be difficult. The leaf structure on an individual plant is often the best clue to species recognition. The genus name, *Arnica*, is derived from the Greek *arnakis*, meaning "lamb's skin," a reference to the woolly bracts and leaf texture on many members of the genus. The species name, *cordifolia*, means "heart-shaped," a reference to the leaves of the plant. A similar species, Mountain Arnica (*A. latifolia*), also known as Broad-Leaved Arnica, inhabits the same habitat. Generally, Mountain Arnica has smaller flowers and round-tipped leaves. Heart-Leaved Arnica occasionally hybridizes with Mountain Arnica, and the resulting plant can be difficult to identify. A number of Native peoples used Arnicas as a poultice for swellings and bruises. Arnicas are said to be poisonous if ingested.

Mountain Goldenrod (Alpine Goldenrod)
Solidago multiradiata

COMPOSITE FAMILY

This erect plant grows from a woody rootstock on dry, open slopes in the subalpine and alpine zones. The leaves are alternate, and often have a reddish appearance. The basal leaves and lower stem leaves are broadly lance- or spoon-shaped, slightly toothed or entire, with hairy margins. The flowers are yellow, and occur in loose or dense, narrow, long clusters atop the stem. Each flower is composed of eight ray florets, surrounding 13 or more disk florets. There are several blunt-ended, reddish, hairy-margined bracts below the flower heads.

The origin of the genus name, *Solidago*, is discussed in the note on Canada Goldenrod (*S. canadensis*), shown on page 233. Goldenrods were often used medicinally to treat a variety of ailments, from headaches, to nausea, to stomach trouble. The species name, *multiradiata*, refers to the numerous ray florets in the flowers. Dwarf Goldenrod (*S. spathulata*) is a related species occurring in similar habitat, but it does not have hairs on the margins of the basal leaves.

Nipplewort
Lapsana communis

COMPOSITE FAMILY

This European import has a solitary, erect, branching stem that stands up to 1.5 m tall, and occurs in fields, along roadsides, and in gardens at low elevations. The stem will exude a milky juice when broken. There are only stem leaves that are numerous, alternate, toothed, and occasionally lobed at the base. The lower leaves have two distinctive small side lobes. The several flower heads have strap-like flowers in an elongated to rounded inflorescence. Each flower has 18 to 20 pale yellow ray flowers with five small teeth at the tips. There are no disk flowers.

The genus name, *Lapsana*, was attributed to the plant by Dioscorides, a Greek physician and pharmacologist who practised in Rome at the time of Nero. Dioscorides travelled extensively in the Greek and Roman world, collecting medicinal substances. He wrote a five-volume work called *De materia medica*, a precursor to modern pharmacopoeias. The species name, *communis*, means "growing in communities." The peculiar common name, Nipplewort, is somewhat contentious. Some say the name comes from the two small side lobes on the lower leaves, contending that they resemble two elongated nipples. Others say the name arises because the closed flower buds resemble nipples. Still others say that the name arises because the plant was used to treat sore or cracked nipples. *Wort* is an Old English name for "herb," or "plant."

Northwest Balsamroot (Deltoid Balsamroot)
Balsamorhiza deltoidea

COMPOSITE FAMILY

Virginia Skilton image

This plant is a perennial herb that grows from a deep taproot, with ascending stems that reach 1 m tall in open areas, on grassy slopes, in open forests and shrubland from low to middle elevations. The leaves are mostly basal, long-stalked, stiff-hairy, triangular, and up to 50 cm long and 20 cm wide, with round teeth on the leaf margins. The flowers resemble sunflowers, and appear in heads at the top of the stems. Each flower has 13 to 21 yellow ray flowers, up to 3 cm long, surrounding yellow disk flowers. There are green, hairy bracts below the flower heads.

The genus name, *Balsamorhiza*, is derived from the Greek *balsamon*, which means "balsam," and *rhiza*, which means "root," alluding to the plant having roots with a balsamic or resinous smell. The species name, *deltoidea*, means "triangular," like Delta, the fourth letter of the Greek alphabet. All parts of the plant are edible and were used as food by Native peoples. The seeds were often dried and ground into flour. Some tribes smoked the leaves like tobacco. The plant also goes by the locally common name of Puget Balsamroot. A very similar plant, Arrow-Leaved Balsamroot (*B. sagittata*), is common and widespread in hot, arid habitat east of the coastal mountains. As the name would imply, it has arrowhead-shaped leaves.

Pale Agoseris (False Dandelion)
Agoseris glauca

COMPOSITE FAMILY

A plant common to moist to dry openings, meadows, and dry open forests, this plant is also known as False Dandelion. The Agoseris shares many characteristics with the Dandelions, including a long taproot, a rosette of basal leaves, a leafless stem, a single yellow flower appearing on a long stalk, and the production of a sticky, milky juice which is apparent when the stem is broken. In fact, this flower is often passed over as just another Dandelion, but upon closer examination several differences are apparent. Agoseris is generally a taller plant than Dandelion, its leaves are longer, and the leaf blades are smooth or faintly toothed rather than deeply incised. The bracts of the Agoseris flower heads are broader than Dandelions, and are never turned back along the stem as they are in Dandelions.

Some Native peoples used the milky juice of the plant as a chewing gum. Infusions from the plant were also used for a variety of medicinal purposes. Agoseris also appears in an orange form (*A. aurantiaca*), shown on page 9.

Pineapple Weed (Disc Mayweed)
Matricaria discoidea

COMPOSITE FAMILY

This branching annual grows up to 40 cm tall along roadsides, in ditches, and on disturbed ground. The stem leaves are alternate and fern-like, with finely dissected, narrow segments. Basal leaves have usually fallen off before flowering occurs. The flowers are several to many composite heads, with greenish to yellow disk florets on a cone-shaped or dome-shaped base. There are no ray florets.

The genus name, *Matricaria*, is derived from the Latin *mater* or *matrix*, meaning "mother" or "womb," and *caria*, meaning "dear," and is a reference to use of the plant in the treatment of uterine infections and other gynecological conditions. When crushed, the leaves and flowers of the plant produce a distinctive pineapple aroma, hence the common name. If you tread on the plant without noticing it first, this aroma will quickly become apparent. Some Native peoples used the plant medicinally, while others used it to scent their homes and baby cradles, or as an insect repellent. Meriwether Lewis collected a sample of the plant in 1806 while he was with the Nez Perce Indians in present-day Idaho. The plant is also known as Rayless Chamomile. Wild Chamomile (*M. perforata*) has similar leaves to Pineapple Weed, but its flowers resemble Ox-Eye Daisy (*Leucanthemum vulgare*), shown on page 85. Wild Chamomile has been used by herbalists for treatment of a variety of conditions.

Smooth Hawksbeard
Crepis capillaria

COMPOSITE FAMILY

This plant is a native of Europe that has been introduced into the region, growing in meadows, pastures, roadsides, and disturbed areas. It grows from a short taproot, sending up a solitary, many-branched, short-hairy stem that is up to 90 cm tall. The basal leaves are lance-shaped, stalked, up to 30 cm long, toothed or pinnately cut with the lobes pointing backward, and softly hairy below. The stem leaves are lance-shaped, clasping, and pointed. The yellow flowers appear in heads in flat- or round-topped clusters. The individual flowers are strap-shaped, unstalked, and made entirely of ray florets. The fruits are round-ribbed brownish achenes, with a short beak at the end.

The genus name, *Crepis*, is derived from the Greek *krepis*, meaning "half boot" or "sandal," and it may be a reference to the deeply cut leaves of some members of the genus, which may suggest the thongs of a sandal. The species name, *capillaria*, means "resembling hair," or "very slender," but whether the reference is to the stems, the stem leaves or the fruits is uncertain. The name Hawksbeard was given to the genus by the botanist Asa Gray, and it is thought to refer to the fruit's resemblance to the bristly feathers that surround a hawk's beak.

Sow Thistle (Perennial Sow Thistle)
Sonchus arvensis

COMPOSITE FAMILY

This is a plant of cultivated fields, roadsides, ditches, and pastures. The flowers have large yellow ray florets similar to dandelion flowers. Sow Thistle is an imported species from Europe. It is not a true thistle. Sow Thistles exude a milky latex when the stem is crushed; true thistles do not.

The common name is derived from the fact that pigs like to eat this plant. The genus name, *Sonchus*, is derived from the Greek word *somphos*, meaning "spongy," a reference to the stems. The species name, *arvensis*, means "of the fields," a reference to the fact that the plant often invades cultivated ground.

Spear-head Senecio (Arrow-leaved Groundsel)
Senecio triangularis

COMPOSITE FAMILY

This leafy, lush perennial herb often grows to 1.5 m tall, and occurs in large clumps in moist to wet, open or partly shaded sites, from the foothills to alpine elevations. The leaves are alternate, spearhead- or arrowhead-shaped, squared off at the base, and tapered to the point. The leaves are numerous and well developed along the whole stem of the plant. They are widest near the middle of the stem and are coarsely sharp-toothed. The flowers occur in flat-topped clusters at the top of the plant, and have five to eight bright yellow ray florets surrounding a disk of bright yellow to orange florets.

The genus name, *Senecio*, is derived from the Latin *senex*, which means "old man." Two opinions emerge as to the intended reference to old man. One says it is because the receptacle to which the flowers are attached is free of hairs, ergo, hairless or bald, like an old man. The other says that the reference is to the grey or white hairs of many members of the genus, ergo, white-haired, like an old man. The species name, *triangularis*, refers to the shape of the leaves, a distinguishing feature of the plant. The common name Ragwort is often applied to members of this genus. It is said to be a reference to the ragged appearance of the leaf margins in many members of the genus. Many members of the genus contain poisonous alkaloids, but livestock seem to find the plants unpalatable. Spear-Head Senecio is often referred to as Giant Ragwort.

Tansy
Tanacetum vulgare

COMPOSITE FAMILY

This plant was introduced from Europe and is common along roadsides, embankments, pastures, fencerows, and disturbed areas. The flowers are yellow and occur in numerous bunches atop multiple stalks. They are flattened and resemble yellow buttons. The leaves are fern-like, dark green, finely dissected, and strong smelling.

Tansies are also known as Button Flowers. The genus name, *Tanacetum*, is derived from the Greek word *athanatos*, meaning "undying" or "immortal," possibly a reference to the long-lasting flowers. In medieval England the plant was placed in shrouds to repel insects and rodents from corpses. It was originally cultivated in North America for its medicinal properties, and it spread from those cultivations. During the Middle Ages a posy of Tansy was thought to ward off the Black Death.

Woolly Sunflower (Oregon Sunshine)
Eriophyllum lanatum

COMPOSITE FAMILY

This plant is a few to many-branched perennial that grows up to 60 cm tall in dry, open, rocky areas from seaside to middle elevations. The plant usually grows in clumps and is white-woolly throughout. The basal leaves are few and usually wilt before blooming commences. The stem leaves are alternate to opposite, smooth on the margins or narrowly lobed, and up to 8 cm long. The flowers are solitary atop the stems, with flower heads consisting of eight to 13 yellow ray flowers up to 2 cm long and yellow disk flowers.

The genus name, *Eriophyllum*, is derived from the Greek *erion*, which means "wool," and *phyllon*, which means "leaf," a reference to the white-woolly appearance of the plant. Redundantly, the specific name, *lanatum*, is Latin meaning "woolly." Meriwether Lewis of the Lewis and Clark expedition collected a specimen of the plant in June 1806 while camped near present-day Kamiah, Idaho.

Bracted Lousewort (Wood Betony)
Pedicularis bracteosa

FIGWORT FAMILY

Gill Ross image

This plant can attain heights of up to 1 m, and is found in subalpine and alpine elevations in moist forests, meadows, and clearings. The leaves are similar to those of ferns – divided into long, narrow, toothed segments – and are attached to the upper portions of the stem of the plant. The flowers vary from yellow to red to purple. The flowers arise from the axils of leafy bracts, and occur in an elongated cluster at the top of the stem. The flowers have a two-lipped corolla, with the upper lip arched downward and the lower lip curving upward, giving the impression of a bird's beak.

The genus name, *Pedicularis*, is from the Latin *pedis*, "louse," and *pediculosus*, "lousy," and plants of this genus are generally referred to as Louseworts. There apparently was a belief at one time that cattle that ate Louseworts were more likely to be afflicted by lice. The species name, *bracteosa*, refers to the leafy bracts below each flower. Louseworts are partially parasitic on the roots of other plants, and derive some of their nutrients from adjacent plants. Herbalists favour the plant as a sedative. The common name Betony is said to derive from an old Iberian word that meant "to cure all ills." The plant is also known by the locally common name Fernleaf.

Butter and Eggs (Toadflax)
Linaria vulgaris

FIGWORT FAMILY

This is a common plant of roadsides, ditches, fields, and disturbed areas that grows up to 1 m tall. It is also known as Toadflax. The leaves are alternate, dark green, and narrow. The flowers are similar in shape to Snapdragons. The bright yellow flowers with orange throats occur in dense, terminal clusters at the tops of erect stems. The corolla is spurred at the base and two-lipped; the upper lip two-lobed, the lower one three-lobed.

The flower takes one of its common names from the yellow and orange tones that resemble the colours of butter and eggs. As to the origin of the other common name, Toadflax, there are two schools of thought. In early English, "toad" meant "false" or "useless," ergo "useless flax" or "false flax" – the leaves of this plant resembling those of Flax. The other school of thought attributes the name "toad" to the resemblance of the flower to that of a toad's mouth. Toadflax was introduced to North America from Europe as a garden plant, but escapees from the garden have become noxious weeds. The plant was used in early Europe to treat jaundice, piles, and eye infections, and was also boiled in milk to make a fly poison. The genus name, *Linaria*, refers to the general similarity of the leaves of this plant to those of Flax. Dalmatian Toadflax (*L. dalmatica*) is a similar species that appears in the same habitat. It has clasping, broadly oval leaves, and larger flowers.

Common Mullein
Verbascum thapsis

FIGWORT FAMILY

A Eurasian import that grows up to 2 m tall, Mullein is quite common along roadsides, gravelly places, and dry slopes. The plant is a biennial, taking two years to produce flowers. In the first year, the plant puts out a rosette of large leaves which are very soft to the touch, much like velvet or flannel. From those leaves surges the strong, sentinel-like stalk in the second year. The small yellow flowers appear randomly from a flowering spike atop the stalk. It appears that at no time do all the flowers bloom together. After flowering, the dead stalk turns dark brown and may persist for many months.

A common name for the plant is Flannel Mullein, a reference to the soft texture of the basal leaves. Mullein is derived from the Latin *mollis*, which means "soft." The dried leaves of the plant were sometimes smoked by Native peoples, and the plant is sometimes called Indian Tobacco. The crushed leaves were often used as a poultice applied to swelling and wounds because the chemicals in the plant soothe irritated tissues and act as a sedative.

Little Monkeyflower (Chickweed Monkeyflower)
Mimulus alsinoides

FIGWORT FAMILY

This plant occurs, often in large patches, in moist, sheltered, rocky areas at low elevations. The stems are freely branching, smooth to slightly hairy, decumbent to erect and up to 25 cm tall. The leaves are opposite, stalked, egg-shaped and irregularly toothed. The flowers are tubular in construction, have long stalks, and appear in the axils of the leaves, usually in pairs. The flowers are two-lipped (bilabiate), with the upper lip being two-lobed and erect, while the lower lip is three-lobed and spreading. The middle lobe on the lower lip is much larger than the lateral lobes, and it has a characteristic red blotch at its base. There is also random spotting in red or maroon inside the flower tube, with the markings typically giving the appearance of a grinning face.

The origin of the genus name, *Mimulus*, is discussed in the note on Yellow Monkeyflower (*M. guttatus*), shown on page 252. The species name, *alsinoides*, means "like the genus *Alsine*," an old name for some plants in the Pink Family. The plant also goes by two locally common names, Chickweed Monkeyflower and Wingstem Monkeyflower. A related species, Red Monkeyflower, (*M. lewisii*) is shown on page 18.

Yellow Monkeyflower
Mimulus guttatus

FIGWORT FAMILY

This plant occurs, often in large patches, along streams, seeps, and in moist meadows. The plant is quite variable, but always spectacular when found. The bright yellow flowers resemble Snapdragons, and occur in clusters. The flowers usually have red or purple dots on the lip, giving the appearance of a grinning face.

The genus name, *Mimulus*, is derived from the Latin *mimus*, meaning "mimic" or "actor," a reference to the "face" seen on the flower. The species name, *guttatus*, means "spotted" or "speckled." The plant is also known by the locally common name Seep Monkeyflower. A related species, Red Monkeyflower, (*M. lewisii*), shown on page 18, also occurs in the region.

Yellow Rattle
Rhinanthus minor (Rhinanthus crista-galli)

FIGWORT FAMILY

Virginia Skilton image

This plant has erect single or partially branched flowering stems that can stand up to 50 cm tall, and is found in low to subalpine elevations on dry plateaus, moist clearings, meadows, and disturbed areas. The leaves are lance-shaped with toothed margins, opposite, and have short stems. The flowers are yellow, and appear in a terminal cluster. Each flower has a two-lipped corolla protruding from an encasing, flattened, inflated calyx. The upper lip of the flower is two-lobed and forms a hood; the lower lip is three-lobed.

Yellow Rattle is a partially parasitic plant that attaches itself to the roots of adjacent plants to obtain water and nutrients. The common name arises because the mature fruit capsules make a rattling noise when shaken. The genus name, *Rhinanthus*, is derived from the Greek *rhinos*, which means "nose" or "snout," and *anthos*, meaning "flower," a reference to the shape of the flower. The plant has several other names that might be locally common, including Money-Grass, Rattlebag, Rattlebox, and Shepherd's-Coffin.

Yellow Sand Verbena
Abronia latifolia

FOUR-O'CLOCK FAMILY

This perennial grows from a deep taproot in loose, shifting beach sand along the coast, away from the surf, just above the tide line. The plant is glandular-hairy and sticky throughout, and its stems trail up to 2 m long, often forming dense mats. The leaves are opposite, ovate, thick, and fleshy, up to 5 cm long and half as wide. The inflorescence occurs in rounded heads (umbels) on stout stalks that are up to 6 cm tall. The umbel contains up to 35 flowers, each a yellow tube with flared mouth that is divided into five lobes. The flowers have a scent that many people associate with salt air.

The genus name, *Abronia*, is derived from the Greek *habros*, which means "graceful" or "delicate," apparently a reference to the bracts below the flowers. Otherwise, the genus name is puzzling, because this plant is quite sturdy and tough. The species name, *latifolia*, is Latin meaning "having wide leaves."

Yellow Heather (Yellow Mountain Heather)
Phyllodoce glanduliflora

HEATH FAMILY

This is a dwarf evergreen shrub that grows up to 30 cm tall, and thrives in subalpine and alpine meadows and slopes near timberline. The flowers, stems, and new growth are covered with small, sticky hairs. The leaves are blunt, needle-like, and grooved on the undersides. The yellowish-green, vase- or urn-shaped flowers are nodding in clusters at the top of the stems.

The genus name, *Phyllodoce*, is explained in the note on Red Heather (*P. empetriformis*), shown on page 38. The species name, *glanduliflora*, refers to the glandular hairs that cover the plant and make it sticky. This plant is not a true heather, but it has been called by that name for so long that it might as well be. Red Heather and Yellow Heather occupy similar habitat, and they will hybridize to produce a variety of colours in the flowers.

Black Twinberry (Bracted Honeysuckle)
Lonicera involucrata

HONEYSUCKLE FAMILY

This plant is a shrub that grows up to 2 m tall in moist woods and along stream banks. The flowers are yellow and occur in pairs, arising from the axils of the leaves. The flowers are overlain by a purple to reddish leafy bract. As the fruit ripens, the bract remains, enlarges, and darkens in colour. The ripe fruits occur in pairs and are black.

The genus name, *Lonicera*, honours the 16th-century German herbalist, physician, and botanist Adam Lonitzer. The species name, *involucrata*, is from the Latin *involucrum*, meaning "wrapper" or "case," and refers to the prominent bracts. Some Native peoples believed that the Black Twinberries were poisonous, and would make one crazy. They are bitter to the taste, but serve as food for a variety of birds and small mammals. The plant is also known by the locally common name of Bracted Honeysuckle.

Glacier Lily (Yellow Avalanche Lily)
Erythronium grandiflorum

LILY FAMILY

This gorgeous lily is one of the first blooms in the spring, often appearing at the edges of receding snowbanks on mountain slopes, thus the common names. The bright yellow flowers appear at the top of a leafless stem, usually solitary, though a plant might have up to three flowers. The flowers are nodding, with six tepals that are tapered to the tip and reflexed, with white, yellow or brown anthers. The leaves, usually two, are attached near the base of the stem and are broadly oblong, glossy and unmarked.

The origin of the genus name, *Erythronium* is explained in the note on Pink Fawn Lily (*E. revolutum*), shown on page 47. The species name, *grandiflorum,* means "large flowered." Glacier Lilies are a favoured food of bears. Bears have been observed digging up the yellow flowers and bulbs, then leaving them to wilt on the ground, returning days later to eat them. Evidently the bears are aware that the bulbs have an increased sweetness after being exposed to the air. Some Native peoples gathered the bulbs as food. The bulbs are inedible when raw, but prolonged steaming converts the indigestible carbohydrates into edible fructose. Drying the bulbs also helps in this process. Glacier Lilies often appear in large numbers, turning the hillsides yellow with their profusion. Two other common local names for the plant are Slide Lily and Dog's Tooth Violet. White Avalanche Lily (*E. montanum*), a similar species, occurs in the alpine and subalpine meadows in the area. Its flowers are white, often with orange centres.

Bird's Foot Trefoil
Lotus corniculatus

PEA FAMILY

This is a low growing, spreading, sprawling, creeping perennial that was introduced from Europe, where it was a pasture plant. Since its introduction, it has spread extensively over the region. It is usually prostrate, but can put up stems 20 cm tall. The leaves are hairless and trifoliate, typical of the pea family. The flowers are yellow, often tinged with red, and occur in a head of three to 12 individual flowers in a cluster at the ends of bare stems, reminiscent of clover blooms.

The genus name, *Lotus*, is from Greek mythology, lotus being a fruit that was said to make those who tasted it forget their homes. How that name was chosen for this genus is a complete mystery, the solution to which is known only by the taxonomist. The species name, *corniculatus*, means "horned," a possible reference to the shape of the flower. The common name is said to arise because the seed pod of the plant resembles a bird's foot. Trefoil may refer to the bract that occurs on the stem immediately under the flower cluster.

Bog Bird's Foot Trefoil
Lotus pinnatus

PEA FAMILY

This native perennial grows from a thick taproot in wet to moist meadows and along streams at low elevations. The stems are sprawling to erect, up to 60 cm long, hollow, and sparsely hairy. The leaves are pinnately compound with five to nine elliptic to egg-shaped leaflets. The inflorescence occurs on a long stem that arises from the leaf axil, and consists of a compact umbel of three to 12 pea-like flowers. The banner and keel on each flower are yellow, the wings white.

The origins of the genus and common names are discussed in the note on Bird's Foot Trefoil (*L. corniculatus*), shown on page 258. The specific name, *pinnatus*, is a reference to the leaf structure of the plant: shaped like a feather. This plant is considered rare in British Columbia, occurring only in sites near Ladysmith and Nanaimo on Vancouver Island. The plant is sometimes referred to as Meadow Bird's Foot Trefoil.

Gorse
Ulex europaeus

PEA FAMILY

Kevin Newell image

This is a non-native, extremely invasive, spiny evergreen shrub that grows up to 2 m tall in open and disturbed ground from the coast to low mountains. The plant grows from a creeping rhizome as well as seed distribution, making it a formidable invader that forces out native vegetation quickly and efficiently. The leaves are simple, stiff, and up to 15 mm long. The plant only has typical trifoliate pea-shaped leaves as a seedling. The flowers are shiny yellow and typical of the pea family. The flowers appear either singly or in clusters at the ends of branches. The fruits are purplish-brown legumes.

The genus name, *Ulex*, is an ancient Latin name applied for centuries to an allied species. Gorse is native to central and western Europe, where it has been used for centuries as hedgerows – a purpose well served by this spiny plant. The plant contains lots of oils and has been used for fuel for centuries. In fact, wildfire appears to promote regeneration of the plant. Gorse is also commonly known as Furze, a name that is said to derive from the Anglo-Saxon *fyrs*, which means "fire," no doubt a reference to using the plant as fuel. The flowers resemble Scotch Broom (*Cytisus scoparius*), shown on page 261, another European invader, but Scotch Broom does not have the prickly nature of Gorse.

Scotch Broom (Broom)
Cytisus scoparius

PEA FAMILY

This is a non-native, aggressively invasive shrub that grows up to 3 m tall in open and disturbed ground from the coast to low mountains. The plant grows from a creeping rhizome as well as through seed distribution, making it a formidable invader that forces out native vegetation quickly and efficiently. The lower leaves are typical trifoliate pea-shaped, but they are undivided above. The flowers are shiny yellow, sometimes tinged with purple or red, and typical of the pea family, occurring one per leaf axil. The fruits are purplish-brown legumes, which open explosively when ripe, casting seeds some distance from the parent plant.

The genus is named after Cythera, one of the Ionic islands where the plant was known to exist. The species name, *scoparius*, means "broom," and indeed, foliage from the plant was used in the manufacture of brooms. Scotch Broom is native to western Europe, but was introduced into western North America by a single planting done near Sooke, British Columbia, in the mid-1800s. From that single, small planting the species has expanded up and down the Pacific coast. Broom contains toxic alkaloids and should not be ingested. The flowers resemble Gorse (*Ulex europaeus*), shown on page 260, another European invader, but Gorse is a spiny shrub, which Scotch Broom is not.

California Poppy
Eschscholzia californica

POPPY FAMILY

This familiar perennial is easily recognized by its saucer-shaped, four-petalled, orange-yellow flowers atop smooth stems that are up to 30 cm tall. The plant grows from a deep taproot, and puts up one to several flowering stems that are spreading to erect. The basal leaves are blue-green, triangular in shape, and three times divided into three leaflets.

The genus name, *Eschscholzia*, honours Dr. Johann Friedrich Gustav von Eschscholtz, a 19th-century Estonian surgeon and botanist who came with two Russian expeditions to the Pacific coast of North America. His name was applied to this plant by his friend and fellow explorer Adelbert von Chamisso. Mountain Buttercup (*Ranunculus eschscholtzii*) is also named for him. This plant is the floral emblem of the State of California, where it is a native plant. It has extended its range northward over time, and is now naturalized in Washington and British Columbia.

Drummond's Mountain Avens (Yellow Mountain Avens)
Dryas drummondii

ROSE FAMILY

This is a plant of gravelly streams and river banks, slopes and roadsides in the foothills and mountains. The yellow flower is solitary and nodding, with black, glandular hairs, blooming on the top of a hairy, leafless stalk. Leaves are alternate, leathery and wrinkly, dark green above and whitish-hairy beneath. The leaves are rounded at the tip, but wedge-shaped at the base. The margins are scalloped and slightly rolled under. The fruit consists of many achenes, each with a silky, golden yellow, feathery plume that becomes twisted around the others into a tight spiral that later opens into a fluffy mass, dispersing the seeds on the wind.

The genus name, *Dryas,* was named for the Dryades, the wood nymphs of Greek mythology. The species name, *drummondii,* honours Thomas Drummond, a Scottish naturalist who accompanied Franklin on his expedition to find the Northwest Passage. Some Native peoples used the plant for medicinal purposes, it being thought that it had healing properties for heart, kidney, and bladder trouble. This small flower likes calcium-rich soil, gravelly streams, and riverbanks, often creating large colonies of flowers. A related species, White Dryad (*D. octopetala*) is shown on page 161.

Large-leaved Avens
Geum macrophyllum

ROSE FAMILY

This is an erect, hairy, tall perennial that grows in moist woods, along rivers and streams and in thickets from low to subalpine elevations. The flowers are bright yellow and saucer-shaped, with five petals. The flowers usually appear at the tip of a tall, slender stem. The basal leaves of the plant occur in a cluster and are pinnately compound, deeply lobed, and toothed. The terminal leaf is rounded, shallowly lobed and much larger than the lateral leaves below it on the stem. The fruits are achenes that have hooks on them, and they will cling to the clothing of passersby and the fur of animals as a seed dispersal mechanism.

The genus name, *Geum*, is from the Greek, *geyo*, meaning "to give a taste of," as the shredded roots of a related Mediterranean species were used. The species name, *macrophyllum*, is a reference to the large terminal leaf of the plant. Native peoples made extensive use of the plant in medicinal concoctions. Leaves and roots of the plant were used in poultices applied to cuts, bruises and boils. A tea made from the plant was used both to prevent conception and to soothe the womb after childbirth.

Sibbaldia

Sibbaldia procumbens

ROSE FAMILY

© V. Skilton

Virginia Skilton image

This is a ground-hugging perennial that forms cushions in the alpine zone. The prostrate stems branch from the base, and terminate in clusters of three leaflets, similar to clover. These leaflets, however, are wedge-shaped, and each has three prominent teeth at the blunt end. White hairs cover both surfaces of the leaflets. The pale yellow flowers are generally saucer-shaped and appear in clusters at the tops of the flowering stems. Each flower is made up of five yellow petals that alternate with five hairy, green sepals. The petals are about half as long as the sepals.

The genus name, *Sibbaldia*, honours Sir Robert Sibbald, an 18th-century Scottish physician and botanist. The species name, *procumbens*, means "prone" or "flat on the ground," a reference to the growth habit of the plant. Some confusion might arise if one encounters Sibbaldia in the same area as some member of the Cinquefoils (*Potentilla* spp). If the plant has three distinct teeth only at the end of the leaflets, it is Sibbaldia.

Silverweed
Potentilla anserina

ROSE FAMILY

This plant is a low, prostrate perennial that grows from thick rootstock and reddish-coloured runners in moist meadows and on riverbanks, lakeshores, and slough margins. The leaves are basal, compound, toothed, and pinnate, with 7–25 leaflets per leaf. Each leaflet is silky-haired and green to silvery on top, lighter underneath. The flowers are bright yellow and solitary on leafless stems, with rounded petals in fives. The sepals are light green and hairy, and appear between the petals.

The common name is derived from the silvery colour of the leaves. The genus name, *Potentilla*, is derived from the Latin *potens*, which means "powerful," an allusion to the supposed medicinal properties of plants of this genus. The species name, *anserina*, means "of or pertaining to geese," and has been variously explained as an allusion to the soft, hairy leaves of the plant being like down, or, alternatively, to the fact that geese might eat the plant in its native habitat. Native peoples used the roots of the plant as food, eating it either raw or cooked. Native peoples also extracted a red dye from the plant and used the runners as cordage material.

Western St. John's Wort
Hypericum scouleri (also *H. formosum*)

ST. JOHN'S WORT FAMILY

Gill Ross image

This perennial appears in moist places from foothills to the alpine zone and grows to 25 cm tall. The leaves are opposite, egg-shaped to elliptical, 1–3 cm long, somewhat clasping at the base, and usually have purplish-black dots along the edges. The bright yellow flowers have five petals and occur in open clusters at the top of the plant. The stamens are numerous and often look like a starburst.

This common name refers to St. John the Baptist. The spots on the leaves were said to ooze blood on the day of his execution. The genus name, *Hypericum*, is the Greek name for a European member of the genus. The species name, *scouleri*, honours John Scouler, a 19th-century Scottish physician and naturalist who collected plant specimens in western North America and the Galapagos Islands. A related plant with similar flowers, Common St. John's Wort (*H. perforatum*), is an introduced noxious weed that occurs in the area. It has narrower lance-shaped leaves. Bog St. John's Wort (*H. anagalloides*) also appears in the area, in wet meadows as the common name would indicate. It is a low-growing, mat-forming plant, and its small yellow flowers lack the black dotting on the margins. Plants in the genus contain compounds that are thought to be potent antiviral agents, and the genus is being studied by AIDS researchers.

Lance-leaved Stonecrop (Spearleaf Stonecrop)
Sedum lanceolatum

STONECROP FAMILY

This fleshy perennial with reddish stems grows up to 15 cm tall on dry, rocky, open slopes and in meadows and rock crevices from low elevations to above timberline. The leaves are numerous, round in cross-section, alternate, fleshy, overlapping and mostly basal. The flowers are bright yellow, star-shaped with sharply pointed petals, and occur in dense, flat-topped clusters atop short stems.

The genus name, *Sedum*, is derived from the Latin *sedere*, which means "to sit," a reference to the plant's low-growing habit. The species name, *lanceolatum*, refers to the plant's lance-shaped leaves. The common name Stonecrop refers to the plant's normal habitat. Some authorities say the plant is edible, while others disagree. Roseroot (*S. rosea*), shown on page 63, is a related species that occurs in subalpine to alpine habitats and has red flowers. Broad-Leaved Stonecrop (*S. spathulifolium*), is also a related species that occurs in the region. It has similar flowers to Lance-Leaved Stonecrop, but its leaves are spoon-shaped and fleshy, and it occurs generally at lower elevations.

Yellow Wood Violet
Viola glabella

VIOLET FAMILY

This beautiful yellow violet occurs in moist woods, and often is found in extensive patches. There are smooth, heart-shaped, serrate leaves on the upper part of the plant stem. The flowers have very short spurs, and the interior of the side petals often exhibit a white beard.

The origin of the genus name, *Viola*, is discussed in the note on Western Long-Spurred Violet (*V. adunca*), shown on page 220. The species name, *glabella*, is Latin meaning "smooth-skinned," a reference to the smooth leaves. The flower is also commonly referred to as Smooth Violet and Stream Violet.

Yellow Pond Lily (Yellow Water Lily)
Nuphar variegatum (also *N. variegata*)

WATER LILY FAMILY

This plant of ponds, lakes, and slow-moving streams is perhaps the most recognizable water plant in the area. This aquatic perennial grows from a thick rootstock, producing cord-like stems. The floating leaves are borne singly on long stems, are up to 15 cm long, waxy on the surface, round and broadly oval, and heart-shaped at the base. The large flowers protrude from the water's surface and are solitary on long stalks, with six sepals that are showy, greenish-yellow on the outside and tinged with red on the inside. Numerous yellow stamens surround a large pistil.

The origin of the genus name, *Nuphar*, is the matter of some dispute among the authorities. Some say it comes from the Persian word *nenuphar*, some say it comes from the Arabic word *naufar*. All agree that both words mean "pond lily." The species name, *variegatum* is Latin meaning "with patches of different colours," a reference to the colours in the sepals. A number of Native peoples employed the plant as food, eating it raw, boiled, baked or ground into flour. Some Native peoples used the plant medicinally to treat venereal disease, make poultices or treat horses. The plant provides cover for fish and food for waterfowl and water mammals.

Glossary

Achene: A dry, single-seeded fruit that does not split open at maturity.

Alkaloid: Any of a group of complex, nitrogen-based chemicals, often found in plants, that are thought to protect the plants against insect predation. Many of these substances are poisonous.

Alternate: A reference to the arrangement of leaves on a stem where the leaves appear singly and staggered on opposite sides of the stem.

Annual: A plant that completes its life cycle, from seed germination to production of new seed, within one year, and then dies.

Anther: The portion of the stamen (the male portion of a flower) that produces pollen.

Axil: The upper angle formed where a leaf, branch, or other organ is attached to a plant stem.

Basal: A reference to leaves where the leaves are found at the base or bottom of the plant, usually near or on the ground.

Berry: A fleshy, many-seeded fruit.

Biennial: A plant that completes its life cycle in two years, normally producing leaves in the first year but not producing flowers until the second year, and then dies.

Bilabiate: In reference to floral construction, having two lips.

Blade: The body of a leaf, excluding the stalk.

Bract: A reduced or otherwise modified leaf that is usually found near the flower or inflorescence of a plant but is not part of the flower or inflorescence.

Bristle: A stiff hair, usually erect or curving away from its attachment point.

Bulb: An underground plant part derived from a short, often rounded shoot that is covered with scales or leaves.

Calcareous: In reference to soils, containing calcium carbonate.

Calyx: The outer set of flower parts, usually composed of sepals.

Capsule: A dry fruit with more than one compartment that splits open to release seeds.

Clasping: In reference to a leaf, surrounding or partially wrapping around a stem or branch.

Cluster: A grouping or close arrangement of individual flowers that is not dense and continuous.

Composite inflorescence: A flower-like inflorescence of the Composite Family, composed of ray and/or disk flowers. Where both ray and disk flowers are present, the ray flowers surround the disk flowers.

Compound leaf: A leaf that is divided into two or many leaflets, each of which may look like a complete leaf, but which lacks buds. Compound leaves may have a variety of arrangements. Pinnate leaves have leaflets arranged like a feather, with attachment to a central stem. Palmate leaves have leaflets radiating from a common point, like the fingers of a hand.

Connate: In reference to leaves, where two leaves are fused at their bases to form a shallow cup, often seen in the Honeysuckle Family.

Corm: An enlarged base or stem resembling a bulb.

Corolla: The collective term for the petals of the flower that are found inside the sepals.

Cultivar: A cultivated variety of a wild plant.

Cyme: A broad, flat-topped flower arrangement in which the inner, central flowers bloom first.

Decumbent: In reference to a plant, reclining or lying on the ground, with tip ascending.

Disk flower: Any of the small tubular florets found in the central clustered portion of the flower head of members of the Composite Family; also referred to as "disk florets."

Dioecious: Having unisex flowers, where male and female flowers appear on separate plants. See also **monoecious.**

Drupe: A fleshy or juicy fruit that covers a single, stony seed inside, e.g., a cherry or peach.

Drupelet: Any one part of an aggregate fruit, e.g., a raspberry or a blackberry, where each such part is a fleshy fruit that covers a single, stony seed inside.

Elliptic: Ellipse-shaped, widest in the middle.

Elongate: Having a slender form, long in relation to width.

Entire: In reference to a leaf, a leaf edge that is smooth, without teeth or notches.

Filament: The part of the stamen that supports the anther. Also can refer to any threadlike structure.

Florescence: Generally the flowering part of a plant; the arrangement of the flowers on the stem; also referred to as "inflorescence."

Floret: One of the small tubular flowers in the central clustered portion of the flower head of members of the Composite Family; also known as "disk flower."

Flower head: A dense and continuous group of flowers without obvious branches or spaces between.

Follicle: A dry fruit composed of a single compartment that splits open along one side at maturity to release seeds.

Fruit: The ripe ovary with the enclosed seeds, and any other structures that enclose it.

Glabrous: In reference to a leaf surface, smooth, neither waxy or sticky.

Gland: A small organ that secrets a sticky or oily substance and is attached to some part of the plant.

Glandular hairs: Small hairs attached to glands on plants.

Glaucous: Having a fine, waxy, often white coating that may be rubbed off; often characteristic of leaves, fruits, and stems.

Hood: In reference to flower structure, a curving or folded, petal-like structure interior to the petals and exterior to the stamens in certain flowers.

Host: In reference to a parasitic or semi-parasitic plant, the plant from which the parasite obtains its nourishment.

Inflorescence: Generally the flowering part of a plant; the arrangement of the flowers on the stem; also referred to as "florescence."

Involucral bract: A modified leaf found just below an inflorescence.

Keel: A ridge or fold, shaped like the bottom of a boat, which may refer to leaf structure, or more often to the two fused petals in flowers that are members of the Pea Family.

Lanate: Covered with woolly hair.

Lance-shaped: In reference to leaf shape, much longer than wide, widest below the middle and tapering to the tip, like the blade of a lance.

Leaflet: A distinct, leaflike segment of a compound leaf.

Linear: Like a line; long, narrow, and parallel-sided.

Lobe: A reference to the arrangement of leaves; a segment of a divided plant part, typically rounded.

Margin: The edge of a leaf or petal.

Mat: A densely interwoven or tangled, low, ground-hugging growth.

Midrib: The main rib of a leaf.

Midvein: The middle vein of a leaf.

Monoecious: A plant having unisex flowers, with separate male and female flowers on the same plant. See also **dioecious**.

Nectary: A plant structure that produces and secretes nectar.

Node: A joint on a stem or root.

Noxious weed: A plant, usually imported, that out-competes with and drives out native plants.

Oblong: Somewhat rectangular, with rounded ends.

Obovate: Shaped like a teardrop.

Opposite: A reference to the arrangement of leaves on a stem where the leaves appear paired on opposite sides of the stem, directly across from each other. See also **palmate**, **pinnate**.

Oval: Broadly elliptic.

Ovary: The portion of the flower where the seeds develop. It is usually a swollen area below the style and stigma.

Ovate: Egg shaped.

Palmate: A reference to the arrangement of leaves on a stem where the leaves spread like the fingers on a hand, diverging from a central or common point. See also **pinnate, opposite.**

Panicle: A branched inflorescence that blooms from the bottom up.

Pappus: The cluster of bristles, scales, or hairs at the top of an achene in the flowers of the Composite Family.

Pencilled: Marked with coloured lines, like the petals on Violets.

Perennial: A plant that does not produce seeds or flowers until its second year of life, then lives for three or more years, usually flowering each year, before dying.

Petal: A component of the inner floral portion of a flower, often the most brightly coloured and visible part of the flower.

Petiole: The stem of a leaf.

Pinnate: A reference to the arrangement of leaves on a stem where the leaves appear in two rows on opposite sides of a central stem, similar to the construction of a feather. See also **opposite, palmate.**

Pistil: The female member of a flower that produces seed, consisting of the ovary, the style, and the stigma. A flower may have one to several separate pistils.

Pistillate: A flower with female reproductive parts but no male reproductive parts.

Pod: A dry fruit.

Pollen: The tiny, often powdery, male reproductive microspores formed in the stamens and necessary for sexual reproduction in flowering plants.

Pome: A fruit with a core, e.g., an apple or pear.

Prickle: A small, sharp, spiny outgrowth from an outer surface.

Raceme: A flower arrangement that has an elongated flower cluster with the flowers attached to short stalks of relatively equal length that are attached to the main central stalk.

Ray flower: One of the outer strap-shaped petals seen in members of the Composite Family. Ray flowers may surround disk flowers or may comprise the whole of the flower head; also referred to as "ray florets."

Receptacle: The enlarged end of a stem to which the flower parts – ray and disk flowers – are attached in members of the Composite Family.

Reflexed: Bent backward, often in reference to petals, bracts, or stalks.

Rhizome: An underground stem that produces roots and shoots at the nodes.

Riverine: Moist habitats along rivers or streams.

Rootstock: Short, erect underground stem from which new leaves and shoots are produced annually.

Rosette: A dense cluster of basal leaves from a common underground part, often in a flattened, circular arrangement.

Runner: A long, trailing, or creeping stem.

Saprophyte: An organism that obtains its nutrients from dead organic matter.

Scape: A flowering stem, usually leafless, rising from the crown, roots, or corm of a plant. Scapes can have a single or many flowers.

Sepal: A leaf-like appendage that surrounds the petals of a flower. Collectively the sepals make up the calyx.

Serrate: Possessing sharp, forward-pointing teeth.

Sessile: Of leaves, attached directly to the base, without a stalk.

Shrub: A multi-stemmed, woody plant.

Simple leaf: A leaf that has a single leaf-like blade, which may be lobed, or divided.

Spike: An elongated, unbranched cluster of stalkless or nearly stalkless flowers.

Spine: A thin, stiff, sharp-pointed projection.

Spur: A hollow, tubular projection arising from the base of a petal or sepal, often producing nectar.

Spurred corolla: A corolla that has spurs.

Stalk: The stem supporting the leaf, flower, or flower cluster.

Stamen: The male member of the flower that produces pollen, typically consisting of an anther and a filament.

Staminate: A flower with male reproductive parts but no female reproductive parts.

Staminode: A sterile stamen.

Standard: The uppermost petal of a typical flower in the Pea Family.

Stigma: The portion of the pistil receptive to pollination; usually at the top of the style, and often sticky or fuzzy.

Stipule: An appendage, usually in pairs, found at the base of a leaf or leaf stalk.

Stolon: A creeping, above-ground stem capable of sending up a new plant.

Style: A slender stalk connecting the stigma to the ovary in the female organ of a flower.

Talus: Loose, fragmented rock rubble usually found at the base of a rock wall; also known as "scree."

Taproot: A stout main root that extends downward.

Tendril: A slender, coiled, or twisted filament with which climbing plants attach to their supports.

Tepals: Petals and sepals that cannot be distinguished from one another.

Terminal: At the top of, such as of a stem or other appendage.

Terminal flower head: A flower that appears at the top of a stem, as opposed to originating from a leaf axil.

Ternate: Arranged in threes, often in reference to leaf structures.

Toothed: Bearing teeth or sharply angled projections along the edge.

Trailing: Lying flat on the ground but not rooting.

Tuber: A thick, creeping underground stem.

Tubular: Hollow or cylindrical, usually in reference to a fused corolla.

Umbel: A flower arrangement where the flower stalks have a common point of attachment to the stem, like the spokes of an umbrella.

Unisexual: Some flowers are unisexual, having either male parts or female parts but not both. Some plants are unisexual, having either male flowers or female flowers but not both.

Urn-shaped: Hollow and cylindrical or globular, contracted at the mouth; like an urn.

Vacuole: A membrane-bound compartment in a plant that is typically filled with liquid and may perform various functions in the plant.

Vein: A small tube that carries water, nutrients, and minerals, usually in reference to leaves.

Viscid: Sticky, thick, and gluey.

Whorl: Three or more parts attached at the same point along a stem or axis, often surrounding the stem; forming a ring radiating out from a common point.

Wings: Side petals that flank the keel in typical flowers of the Pea Family.

Photographic Credits

All photographs are by the author except those listed below, with sincere thanks by the author to the photographers for their gracious permission to use their work in this book.

Dave Ingram
Gold Star p. 235
Mist Maiden p. 175
Salal (fruit) p. 39
Silver-Back p. 89

Kevin Newell
Dove's-Foot Crane's-Bill p. 23
Gorse p. 260
Indian Plum (fruit) p. 153

Jim Riley
Beach Carrot p. 78
Buck-Bean p. 67
Buckbrush p. 68
Gnome Plant p. 31
Large-Flowered Collomia p. 142
Musk Mallow p. 48
One-Flowered Cancer Root p. 182
Slender Waterleaf p. 177
Spreading Phlox p. 143
Western Corydalis p. 21

Gill Ross
Bracted Lousewort p. 248
Creeping Raspberry p. 151
Western St. John's Wort p. 267

Doug Skilton
Columbia Lewisia p. 147
Poque (both images) p. 227
Northern Riceroot p. 205
White Heather p. 108

Virginia Skilton
Alaska Rein-Orchid p. 133
Broad-Leaved Arrowhead p. 174
Chocolate Lily p. 202
Coast Penstemon p. 191
Copperbush p. 29
Davidson's Penstemon p. 192
King Gentian p. 196
Large Round-Leaved Orchid p. 136
Mock Orange p. 113
Mountain Marsh Marigold p. 76
Northwest Balsamroot p. 240
Paintbrush p. 20
Roundleaf Sundew p. 172
Sibbaldia p. 265
Thrift p. 56
Vanilla Leaf p. 66
Western Tea Berry p. 107 *(both images)*
Yellow Rattle p. 253

Roman Stone
Candy-Stick p. 28

Tracy Utting
Purple Saxifrage p. 219

BIBLIOGRAPHY

Clark, L.J. and J. Trelawny (ed.), 1973, 1976, 1998. *Wildflowers of the Pacific Northwest.* Harbour Publishing, Madeira Park, British Columbia.

Cormack, R.G.H., 1977. *Wild Flowers of Alberta.* Hurtig Publishers, Edmonton, Alberta.

Kershaw, L., A. MacKinnon and J. Pojar, 1998. *Plants of the Rocky Mountains.* Lone Pine Publishing, Edmonton, Alberta.

Parish, R., R. Coupé, and D. Lloyd (eds.), 1996. *Plants of Southern Interior British Columbia.* Lone Pine Publishing, Edmonton, Alberta.

Phillips, H.W., 2001. *Northern Rocky Mountain Wildflowers.* Falcon Publishing Inc., Helena, Montana.

Phillips, H.W., 2003. *Plants of the Lewis & Clark Expedition.* Mountain Press Publishing Co., Missoula, Montana.

Scotter, G.W., H. Flygare, 1986. *Wildflowers of the Canadian Rockies.* Hurtig Publishers Ltd., Edmonton, Alberta.

Vance, F.R., J.R. Jowsey, J.S. McLean, and F.A. Switzer, 1999. *Wildflowers across the Prairies.* Greystone Books, Vancouver, British Columbia.

Wilkinson, K. 1999. *Wildflowers of Alberta.* University of Alberta Press and Lone Pine Publishing, Edmonton, Alberta.

INDEX

Neil Jennings is an ardent fly fisher, hiker, and photographer who loves "getting down in the dirt" pursuing his keen interest in wildflowers. For 22 years he was a co-owner of Country Pleasures, a fly-fishing retailer in Calgary, Alberta. He fly fishes extensively, both in fresh and saltwater, and his angling pursuits usually lead him to wildflower investigations in a variety of venues. He has taught fly-fishing-related courses in Calgary for over 20 years, and his photographs and writings on the subject have appeared in a number of outdoor magazines. Neil has previously written three books on western wildflowers – *Uncommon Beauty*, *Alpine Beauty*, and *Prairie Beauty* – all published by Rocky Mountain Books. He is also the author of *Behind the Counter*, a book on fly fishing, also published by Rocky Mountain Books. Neil lives in Calgary with Linda, his wife of over 30 years. They spend a lot of time outdoors together chasing fish, flowers, and, as often as possible, grandchildren.

Central Beauty

Wildflowers and Flowering Shrubs of the
Southern Interior of British Columbia

By Neil L. Jennings

Central Beauty explores the wildflowers and flowering shrubs
commonly found in the portions of British Columbia typically
known as the southern interior - very roughly an east-west line
drawn through Williams Lake, B.C. The southern limit of the
area extends into the states of Washington, Idaho and Montana.

ISBN: 978-1-897522-03-5
Price: $26.95
Pages: 320 pages. 5" x 8". Paperback
Illustrations: colour photos throughout

Central
Beauty

Wildflowers and Flowering Shrubs of the
Southern Interior of British Columbia

Neil L. Jennings

Rocky
Mountain Books

Alpine Beauty

*Alpine and Subalpine Wildflowers of the
Canadian Rockies and Columbia Mountains*

By Neil L. Jennings

Alpine Beauty explores the wildflowers and flowering shrubs
commonly found in the subalpine and alpine environments in
the Rocky Mountains of western Canada. Due to harsh weather
conditions, the plants that exist at higher elevations are generally
different than those at lower elevations. In this environment,
low shrub and herb communities become the rule.

ISBN: 978-1-894765-83-1
Price: $22.95
Pages: 224 pages. 5" x 8". Paperback
Illustrations: colour photos throughout

Uncommon Beauty
Wildflowers and Flowering Shrubs of Southern Alberta and Southeastern British Columbia

By Neil L. Jennings

Uncommon Beauty explores the wildflowers and flowering shrubs of a large area from Jasper down to Creston, over to Glacier National Park in Montana, and up through Lethbridge and Edmonton.

ISBN: 978-1-894765-75-6
Price: $22.95
Pages: 256 pages. 5" x 8". Paperback
Illustrations: colour photos throughout

Prairie Beauty
Wildflowers of the Canadian Prairies

By Neil L. Jennings

Prairie Beauty explores the wildflowers and flowering shrubs commonly found in the prairie environment of western Canada.

ISBN: 978-1-894765-84-8
Price: $24.95
Pages: 248 pages. 5" x 8". Paperback
Illustrations: colour photos throughout